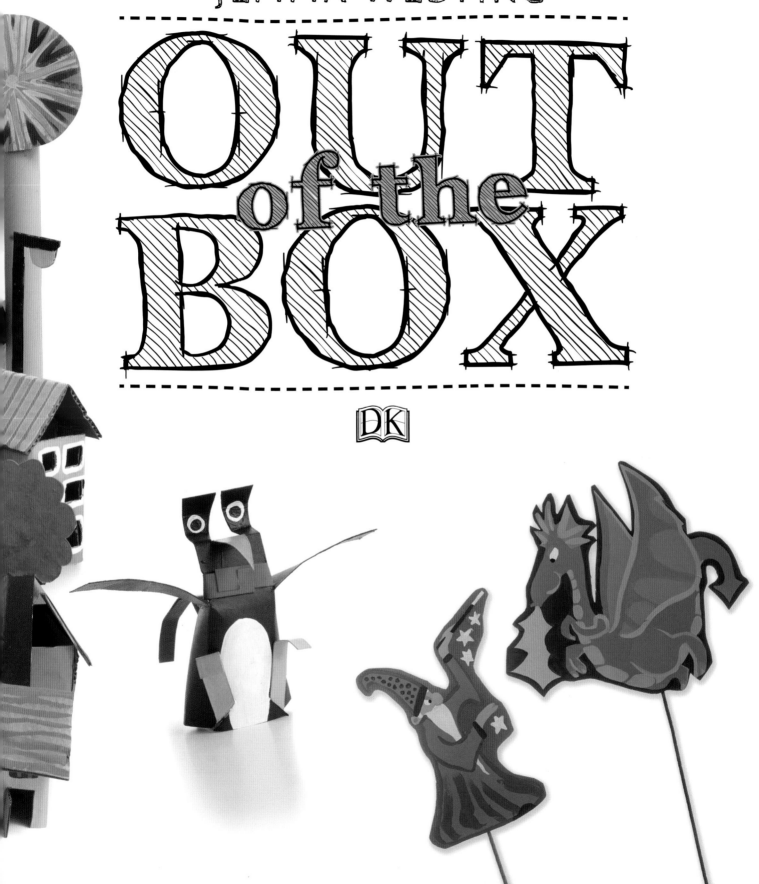

JEMMA WESTING

OUT of the BOX

DK

Senior art editor Amy Child
Project editors Suhel Ahmed, Lili Bryant
Designers Laura Gardner, Mik Gates, Alex Lloyd, Sean Ross
Editors Sarah Edwards, Laura Sandford
US Senior editor Shannon Beatty
US editor Jill Hamilton
Design assistant Edward Byrne

Managing editor Daniel Mills
Managing art editor Anna Hall
Producer, pre-production David Almond
Producer Anna Vallarino
Jacket design development manager Sophia MTT
Jacket editor Claire Gell
Senior jacket designer Mark Cavanagh
Jacket designer Jemma Westing

Publisher Andrew Macintyre
Associate publishing director Liz Wheeler
Art director Karen Self
Publishing director Jonathan Metcalf

Author and model creator Jemma Westing
Photographer Dave King
Photography art direction Jane Ewart
Illustrator Edward Byrne

First American Edition, 2017
Published in the United States by DK Publishing
345 Hudson Street, New York, New York 10014

Copyright © 2017 Dorling Kindersley Limited
DK, a Division of Penguin Random House LLC
17 18 19 20 21 10 9 8 7 6 5 4 3 2 1
001-299504-May/2017

DK books are available at special discounts when purchased in bulk for sales
promotions, premiums, fund-raising, or educational use. For details, contact:
DK Publishing Special Markets, 345 Hudson Street, New York, New York 10014
SpecialSales@dk.com

Printed and bound in China

A WORLD OF IDEAS:

SEE ALL THERE IS TO KNOW
www.dk.com

⚠ IMPORTANT NOTE TO PARENTS

The activities in this book may require adult help and supervision, depending
on your child's age and ability. Always ensure that your child uses tools that
are appropriate to their age, and offer help and supervision as necessary
to keep them safe. The publisher cannot accept any liability for injury, loss,
or damage to any property or user following suggestions in this book.

CONTENTS

Use cardboard boxes and sheets for projects that need sturdy cardboard.

Cardboard sheets

Cardboard tubes

Cardboard tubes come in a variety of sizes.

NOTE FROM THE AUTHOR

Cardboard is an incredibly versatile craft material. You can fold it, roll it, cut it, tape it, and paint it to make exciting things such as colorful lizards, balancing butterflies, robot costumes, and much more. The projects in this book were inspired by the activities at BrilliantBuilds—a workshop I set up to offer young families an encouraging space where they can inspire one another and be creative together. Now you can enjoy these projects, too. Get friends and family members involved in the larger projects and discover how much fun recycling can be!

JEMMA WESTING

Tissue boxes and cereal boxes are a great source of thin cardboard for smaller projects.

Thin cardboard boxes

Egg cartons provide a unique cardboard shape to build with.

Egg carton

Colored envelopes
are a good source of
colored paper.

GETTING
STARTED

The projects in this book use cardboard packaging that you can find lying around the house. The book will show you how to make recycling fun by building exciting, interactive models that you can play with afterward. You'll find a list of the materials and tools required at the start of each project. Once you have everything you need, simply follow the instructions and see your wonderful creations come together!

Tracing paper

White paper

Use tracing paper or thin white paper to copy templates for making more complex shapes.

TYPES OF CARDBOARD

Cardboard comes in many different forms, shapes, and sizes. A box provides a great structure for making many of the models, and cardboard tubes (taken from rolls of wrapping paper and paper towels) provide ready-made cylindrical shapes. Molded cardboard, such as egg boxes, shoe formers, and furniture corner caps offer more interesting shapes, and cereal boxes are an ideal source of thin card. Try not to throw away any scraps, but store them in a special "off-cuts" box, as they might come in handy for another project.

IGNORE THE PRINT

Cereal and tissue boxes will have designs and logos on them. Don't worry. You can paint over these when you decorate your model, or you might decide to keep them because they give your build a unique appeal.

OTHER BITS AND PIECES

Some projects require additional material besides cardboard, usually for adding the final touches. Once again, these should be easy to find, but make your own alternatives if you are struggling to find them.

INSIDE YOUR
TOOLBOX

The great thing about building out of cardboard is that you don't need to invest in specialized tools and equipment. Everything you need is probably in your desk drawer already, so you should be ready to start right away. It is important that you use the right kind of tape in each project, and have scissors, rulers, and paintbrushes of varying sizes so you can make the smaller decorative builds as well as the large-scale models.

Decorate your models with glitter to add sparkle to them.

Check which type of tape you need before starting a project.

Double-sided tape

Sticky tape

Scissors

Strong tape

Glue

Thread

String

Pencil

Rulers

Colored pencils

Paints

Paintbrushes

Use a broad
paintbrush to decorate
your larger models.

Felt tip pens offer
an easier option
for coloring in
intricate patterns.

Felt tip pens

Use acrylic paints to
decorate your models.

Adhesive putty

Paints

CARDBOARD SKILLS

The different ways of cutting, shaping, and connecting cardboard are all very similar to each other, so once you have learned the basic principles, you can apply them to all the projects. The projects get more challenging as the book goes on, so if you're a beginner, start with the first project and see your skills grow as you work your way through.

Each project begins with a panel that includes a useful tip and a dial that tells you how challenging the project is.

Nice and quick! Make several for an eye-catching display.

Difficulty level: Easy

DRAWING
You'll mostly be drawing straight lines and basic shapes. For circles you can draw around a cup, plate, or any other circular object.

CUTTING
Use a small pair of scissors to cut thin cardboard and more intricate shapes, and larger scissors to cut thick pieces of cardboard.

A sharp pencil is a great tool for piercing holes.

Adhesive putty

MAKING HOLES
For neat, round holes, pierce cardboard with the tip of a pencil with an eraser or adhesive putty on the other side so you don't poke the surface below.

CUTTING OUT SHAPES
To cut out a shape, use a sharp pencil to pierce the cardboard, while holding adhesive putty on the other side to protect your fingers. Then cut the shape out.

ROLLING

To make a tube, lay your cardboard piece on a flat surface and roll it into the size you want. Then trim off any excess cardboard and tape the edge to secure the shape.

BENDING

You can use your hands to bend cardboard into all kinds of curved shapes and then secure it with tape. Take your time when you bend thick cardboard.

SCORING AND FOLDING

To fold thick cardboard, use the blunt tip of your scissors to score along the fold line first, and always score on the outside of the fold.

FLAPS AND TABS

Flaps and tabs are useful for connecting the edges of two cardboard pieces to form a right-angle join. You'll be using this method frequently.

Make tabs when you need to stick cardboard pieces together.

TAPING

Sticky tape is fine for the small projects, but strong tape is more suitable for making the larger objects because the joins need to be stronger.

GLUING

For creating neat, invisible joins in the smaller decorative objects, use glue instead of tape, especially to stick cardboard onto cardboard.

Use strong tape to secure the balloon stand to your work surface.

BALLOON STAND

For the projects that involve making hats, masks, and headdresses, you can either build directly around your head, which might be tricky unless you have help, or create a head shape to build on. If you decide to use the balloon stand featured throughout this book, blow up a balloon to roughly the size of your head and place it on a cardboard base that is about as wide as your neck.

MAKE YOUR OWN BOX

If you can't find the right size box for any of the projects, you can always make your own box. First, cut out a cardboard rectangle, fold it to make a rectangular tube, and secure it with tape. Then cut out two cardboard squares and tape them over the ends of the tube.

TEMPLATES FOR TRACING

The templates at the back of the book are there to help you draw more complex shapes. If you need to use a template for a project, the instructions will tell you which page to find it on. Turn to the relevant page, trace the template onto plain paper or tracing paper, and cut it out. Then, lay the paper cutout on cardboard and draw around it for the exact shape you need. Occasionally, you'll be instructed to flip the template over to make a symmetrical shape.

DEALING WITH MISHAPS!

If you accidentally tear a bit of cardboard or cut it too short, you could tape it together, glue it back on, or just remake the piece. Similarly, if you don't like the color you've used for decorating, wait until it's dry and then paint over it. Mistakes will happen, but don't let that put you off—work through them!

NOW TRY THIS

Most projects in this book have a section at the end called "Now Try This," which will show you alternative ways to decorate your models, or things you can add to them to make them extra special. You can even combine parts of two or more different projects! For example, this book will show you how to turn your penguins from the Penguin Family (page 88) into competitors in the game Racing Rabbits (page 44).

Paint the racetrack in icy colors.

Add a paper tube to your penguins so they can join in the racing game.

TUBE OWLS

Did you know that there are more than 200 species of owls? Now you can make your very own collection of cute, colorful owls. Give them huge eyes to help them spot their prey, and pointed talons so they can perch in the trees!

Press the top of the tube down to give your owl pointed ear tufts.

Decorate your owls in bright, contrasting colors.

Paint large, round eyes onto your owls.

HOW TO MAKE
TUBE OWLS

It's really quick and easy to transform a cardboard tube into one of these lovable owls. Making a few simple cuts into the tube will give your owl feet, a beak, and wings!

All you need to do is **cut, fold, and paint** a cardboard tube.

Difficulty level: Easy

YOU WILL NEED

Pencil

Paints

Scissors

Cardboard tube

Paintbrushes

Make sure you've cut the tube down to size if it's too long.

1 First, make the owl's **feet**. Gently flatten your tube and draw four short lines, spaced apart as shown. Make cuts along all four lines.

2 The cuts that you have made will create two flaps. Fold these flaps outward and away from the tube to make the owl's feet.

3 Now that you have folded the feet over, trim around the base of the tube. Cut away any cardboard that is below the level of the feet.

Draw zigzag lines for talons.

4 To finish making the feet, draw zigzag lines on the end of each foot. Carefully cut along the lines to give your owl nice pointed **talons**.

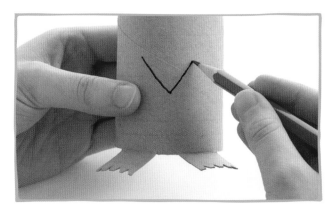

5 Next, make the owl's **beak**. Using a pencil, carefully draw a V shape in the center of the tube.

6 Squeeze the tube a little to help you cut along the two lines. Then pry out the beak and gently fold it up away from the tube, making sure it doesn't tear.

The pressed-down ends of the tube give your owl its ears.

7 To make the owl's **head**, press down the front and back edges of the top of the tube. Then fold them inward to form a curved head shape.

8 Finally, draw the **features** of your owl with a pencil. Then paint them on in bright colors, using a fine paintbrush for any detailed decoration.

NOW TRY THIS

Add **wings** to your owls. To do this, cut V shapes on either side of the tube, following the instructions in **step 6**.

Add feather details.

Gently curve the wings away from the body.

RING TOSS CHALLENGE

Do you love fairground games, but hardly ever get to play them? Why not create your own ring toss game at home? Invite your friends to play, then work on perfecting your aim.

Try to throw all the rings over the pins.

Make the pins different shapes and sizes.

You can make the target board as big and complex as you want to.

HOW TO MAKE
RING TOSS CHALLENGE

The game is very easy to make and will provide hours of fun for you and your friends. Make sure you store the board inside so you can use it again and again!

You will need a **very large piece of cardboard** and lots of bright paint colors.

Difficulty level: Easy

Adhesive putty

Large cardboard sheet

Ruler

Scissors

Pencil

Paints

Paintbrushes

Make sure the pins are far enough apart and small enough for the rings to fit over them.

1 To make your **target board**, draw the outline of the board on a sheet of cardboard and add sloping flaps on either side. These will make the board stand up.

2 Carefully cut out your target board with scissors. Make sure you don't cut off the sloping flaps!

Don't cut here.

Don't cut here.

3 Use a ruler and the tips of your scissors to score both sloping ends of the target board. Fold them back to create flaps to stand your board up.

Score here, too.

4 It's time to decorate the board. Paint the stand one color and each pin a different color, so they stand out.

Make sure the flaps are stable and the stand is not near anything fragile.

5 Place your ring template from page 134 on a piece of cardboard and draw around it. Repeat the process to draw as many rings as you want.

6 Cut the rings out. Cut around the outside first, then place the adhesive putty underneath, pierce the center of the ring with a sharp pencil, and cut it out.

7 Paint the rings and leave them to dry. You can make them any color you like. You could even add patterns like stripes or dots to your set.

8 The ring toss board is ready. Find some friends and try it out. If you want to make things competitive, paint different point values on the pins and see who can reach 100 points first.

Be careful not to bend the pins over when you set the stand up.

Stand about five paces away and try to throw the rings over the pins.

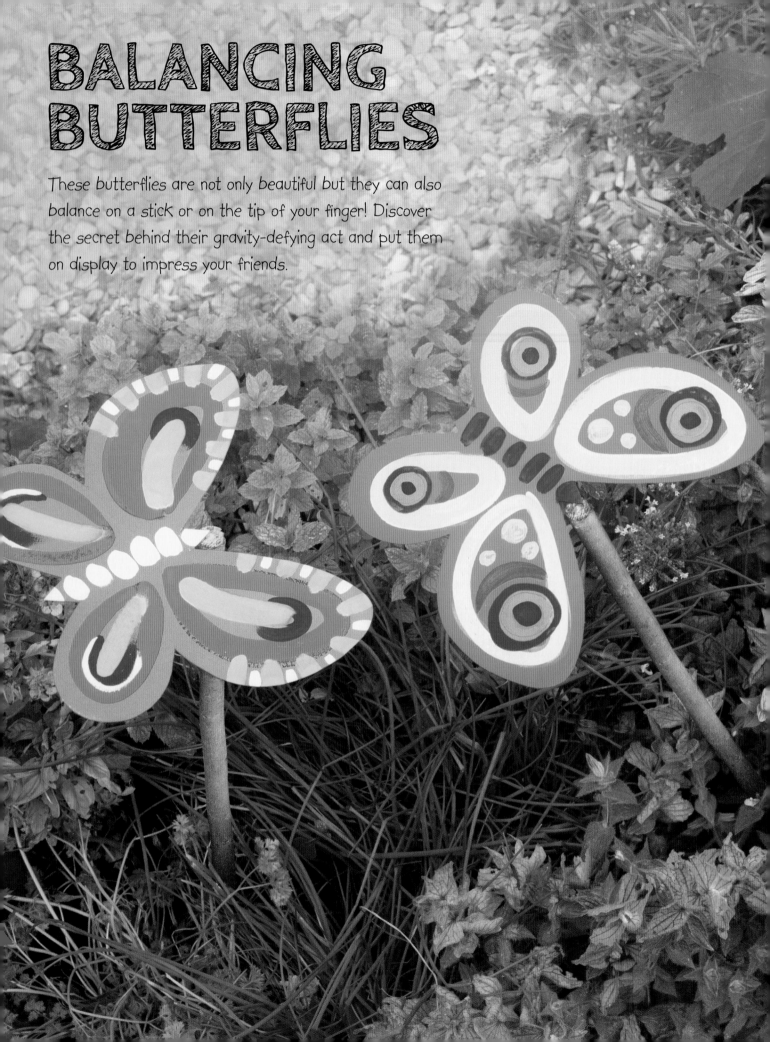

BALANCING BUTTERFLIES

These butterflies are not only beautiful but they can also balance on a stick or on the tip of your finger! Discover the secret behind their gravity-defying act and put them on display to impress your friends.

HOW TO MAKE
BALANCING BUTTERFLIES

Use the template on page 135 to draw the butterfly and decorate it with bright colors and pretty patterns. Once finished, add sticky tack to each wing, then pick up the butterfly and watch it balance on the tip of your finger!

A **quick and easy** project. Make several butterflies for a stunning display!

Difficulty level:
Easy

YOU WILL NEED

Paints

Thin cardboard box

Adhesive putty

Paintbrushes

Scissors

Pencil

1 Using a pair of scissors, cut out a large rectangle of thin card. The front or back panel of a cereal box is the ideal size.

2 Lay your **butterfly wing** template from page 135 on the card and draw around it, leaving room to draw the other half of the butterfly.

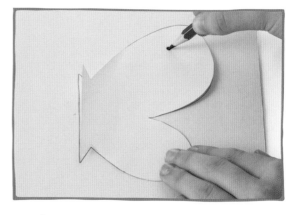

3 Put the tip of your pencil on the dot on the template, twist and push down hard to pierce the template and make a dot on the cardboard below.

4 Flip the template over and draw around it to complete the butterfly shape. Then push your pencil tip into the hole and mark a dot on this wing too.

5 Carefully cut out your butterfly. The wings need to be symmetrical for your butterfly to balance, so cut as close to the lines as possible.

Carefully push a pencil through the middle of the adhesive putty.

6 Now use brightly colored paint to decorate the side of the butterfly without the two dots, adding beautiful patterns. Let the paint dry.

7 Roll two identical disks of adhesive putty. Make a hole in the middle of each one with a pencil. Then use the pencil tip to line up the hole in each disk with the dot on the wing and fix it on.

8 Your butterfly is ready! Rest it on a point (like a stick, table corner, or the end of your finger) and watch it perform its awesome balancing act!

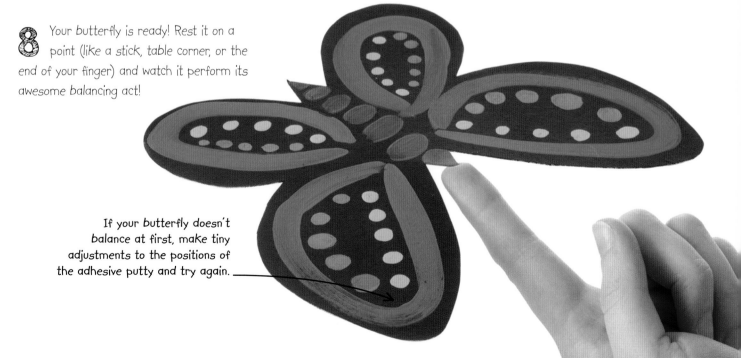

If your butterfly doesn't balance at first, make tiny adjustments to the positions of the adhesive putty and try again.

Paint your board in a dark color so your monsters stand out.

FEED THE MONSTERS

These monsters are ready for their dinner, and it's up to you to feed them! Create a huge board full of brightly colored monsters with wide-open mouths and sharp teeth. Then put your skills to the test and see how many monsters you can feed in a minute, or challenge a friend to see who can feed the most monsters.

FEED ME!

HOW TO MAKE
FEED THE MONSTERS

You'll need a huge sheet of cardboard for this project, so you can fill it with lots of hungry monsters. Make sure you also have enough cardboard to make two identical stand pieces, so that your board stays upright when you feed the monsters.

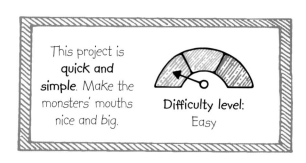

This project is **quick and simple**. Make the monsters' mouths nice and big.

Difficulty level: Easy

YOU WILL NEED

Pencil

Paints

Large cardboard sheet

Paintbrushes

Sticky tape

Strong tape

Scissors

Colored paper

Ruler

1 On a large sheet of cardboard, draw lots of **monster faces** with wide open mouths and sharp teeth.

2 Carefully cut out holes where you have drawn the monsters' **mouths**. You might want to ask an adult to help.

Draw this horizontal line on both pieces for your stand.

3 Make the **stand** for your board. Take a square piece of cardboard and draw three lines on it as shown above.

4 Cut along the diagonal line. Then, use your first stand piece as a template to create another.

5 Score along the horizontal lines on both stand pieces to make tabs. Fold the tabs upward.

6 Tape the tabs to each side of the board at the back. The diagonal edge of each stand piece should touch the floor.

7 To make your **paper balls**, scrunch up colored paper into tight balls and wrap them in sticky tape.

8 Decorate your **board** and let the paint dry. Then stand it upright and you're ready to play!

Paint your monsters in bold colors.

NOW TRY THIS

Make one big monster by cutting a single monster mouth out of a cardboard box. Take the rings from the Ring Toss Challenge on page 21, and try to feed the monster yummy hoops. Use more cardboard to add arms or hair if you like.

Paint the whole box.

Use more card to add details to your mega-monster.

Cut out one big hole for the mouth.

FUNKY FLOWERS

This beautiful spray of bright, exotic flowers makes a fantastic decoration for your desk or windowsill. Or you can use them to make a hanging garland to bring color to any room.

HOW TO MAKE
FUNKY FLOWERS

These flowers have three rings of petals: two made from a cardboard tube, and one cut from a template. The more evenly spaced the petals are, the neater your flowers will look, so measure and cut carefully.

A **quick project** that won't take up too much time or space!

Difficulty level: Easy

YOU WILL NEED

Thin cardboard box

White paper

Scissors

Pencil

Paints

Paintbrushes

Glue

Sticky tape

Wooden sticks

Ruler

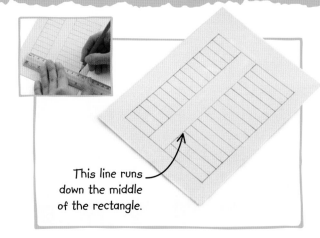

This line runs down the middle of the rectangle.

1 Use a pencil and ruler to draw the shape shown above on a piece of card. Make sure the rectangular strips are longer on one side of the piece than on the other side.

Line up the end with the nearest pencil line.

2 Cut out the rectangle, then roll it into a tube with the pencil lines facing out. Use sticky tape to hold the tube together.

Avoid cutting into the central gap.

3 Use scissors to cut along the lines on each side of the tube. Be careful not to cut into the gap in the middle, or your flower will fall apart.

Fold here.

4 Gently bend the shorter set of strips outward, so they form curves. These will become the **middle ring of petals** on your flower.

5 To create the **inner ring of petals**, push the longer strips through the tube so that they stick out at the other side. Fold the bases of the strips along the rim to keep them in place.

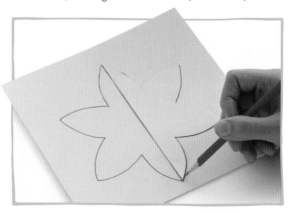

6 Squeeze a piece of paper up into a tight ball, then wedge it securely into the center of the tube. You may need to add a little glue to the outside of the ball of paper to hold it in place.

7 To make the **outer ring of petals**, copy the petal template from page 135 onto a piece of thin cardboard. Turn the template over, then draw around it again to make a complete ring of petals.

8 Use scissors to cut out the complete outer ring of petals. Don't cut down the middle!

9 To fix your flower together, put a dab of glue in the center of your outer petal shape, then stick the rest of the flower securely on top.

11 Now it's time to paint your flower. Choose a main color for each section, then add details and patterns on top.

10 Press down on the *ball of paper* in the center of your flower to make sure all the pieces are securely stuck together.

12 To make the **stalk**, use sticky tape to fix a stick or straw to the back of your flower. Your brilliant bloom is now ready to display in a vase or flowerbed.

Look at pictures of real flowers for inspiration.

Try using a vibrant color for the center of the flower.

NOW TRY THIS

Instead of putting your flowers on stalks, try creating a *beautiful floral garland*. Make five or six flowers and decorate them any way you like for an eye-catching garland! Then use a pencil to pierce a small hole in one of the outer petals on each flower. Thread a length of string through the holes and tie the ends together to complete your garland.

Thread string through holes in the petals.

Arrange your flowers to make a pattern.

CARDBOARD THEATER

Put on an amazing show in your very own puppet theater! Transform a cardboard sheet into a beautiful old-fashioned theater with a wooden floor and a colorful stage. Then, push your imagination to its limits and create an all-star cast of characters to bring your story to life.

Add trees from Cardville City (page 94) and towers from the Adventure Castle (page 80) to make a three-dimensional scene.

Make dragons, wizards, or any characters you like for your show!

CARDBOARD THEATER

To make this traditional puppet theater, you'll be turning a sheet of cardboard into a stage. Then, once you've painted your theater and made some sturdy brackets to hold it up, you can use cardboard and sticks to make a cast of characters for your show.

Take your time
drawing the intricate theater design, or simplify it if you want to.

Difficulty level:
Easy

YOU WILL NEED

Paints

Paintbrushes

Scissors

Ruler

Wooden sticks

Pencil

Thin cardboard

Cardboard sheets

Glue

1 On a piece of cardboard, draw a large rectangle for your **stage**. Then copy the stage outline shown above.

2 Now draw patterns around the stage. Work outward, and try to make your design look the same on each side.

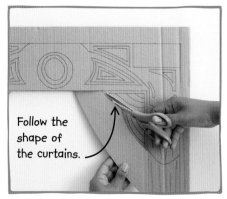

Follow the shape of the curtains.

3 Cut out a space in the center. Don't forget to follow the shape of your curtains.

4 Score the horizontal line along the bottom of the rectangle so you can fold up the stage **floor**.

5 Now decorate your stage. Paint the floor orange and add brown lines to create a wooden effect.

6 Make **brackets** to hold up the stage. Draw a square and divide it in half with a diagonal line. Add tabs to each side.

7 Cut the shape out and cut along the diagonal line to create two brackets. Score and fold the tabs.

8 Paint the brackets in colors that match the stage. Make one tab the same color as the stage floor.

9 Now fold up the stage floor. Glue your brackets to each side of the stage, fixing the orange tabs to the floor.

10 Draw any **characters** you like on card (or use pictures from magazines), paint them, and tape a wooden stick to the back of them.

Bring characters to life with fun stories.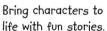

11 Place your theater on a surface that you can sit under so that you are out of sight. If the theater falls over, secure it with adhesive putty. Hold the sticks to move your characters around the stage.

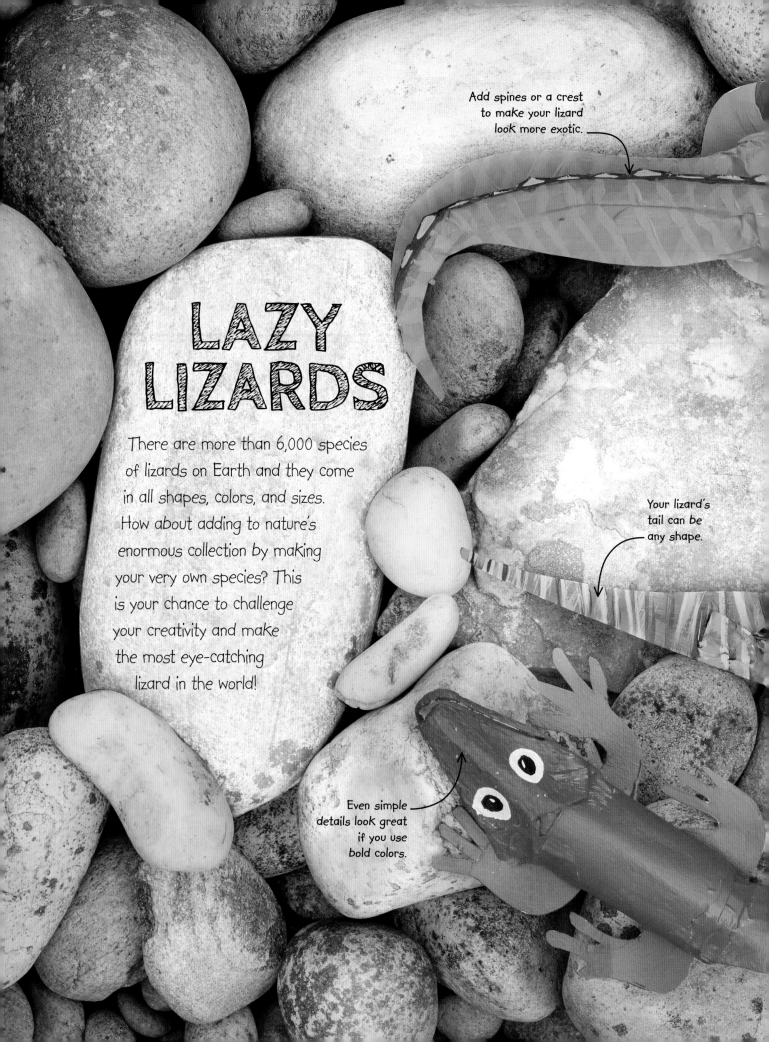

LAZY LIZARDS

There are more than 6,000 species of lizards on Earth and they come in all shapes, colors, and sizes. How about adding to nature's enormous collection by making your very own species? This is your chance to challenge your creativity and make the most eye-catching lizard in the world!

Add spines or a crest to make your lizard look more exotic.

Your lizard's tail can be any shape.

Even simple details look great if you use bold colors.

Add glitter to
make your lizard
stand out.

An egg carton
provides a cone
shape for the
lizard's head.

HOW TO MAKE
LAZY LIZARDS

These laid-back reptiles are quick and easy to make. You could make several eye-catching lizards and decorate them all differently, so that each one is unique and full of character.

Quick and easy to make, but **be as creative as you want** with the decoration.

Difficulty level:
Easy

YOU WILL NEED

Thin cardboard box

Egg carton

Sticky tape

Scissors

Pencil

Paints

Paintbrushes

Ruler

1 First make the lizard's **head**. Cut a cone out of the egg carton by cutting around the base of one of the central dividers.

Leave a gap between the slit and edge.

Repeat cut below.

2 To add the **mouth**, cut a slit through the point of the cone on both sides. Don't cut all the way to the edge. Then, gently pull the slits apart.

3 Now make the lizard's **body**. Draw a rectangle on a piece of cardboard from your box, using a ruler to keep the lines straight. Cut out the rectangle.

Fix tape to the edge before you begin rolling.

4 Roll the rectangle into a tube. Check that it is wide enough to fit snugly into the hollow end of the head. Tape the edge of the tube to secure it.

5 Push the *body* firmly into the head section. Fix it in place by sticking strips of sticky tape where the head and body join, on either side.

Bend the edge of the tail gently to curve it.

6 Now take another thin piece of cardboard and draw and cut out the lizard's **tail**. It can be curly, straight, wiggly, or even a zigzag shape!

7 Bend the end of the tail to give it a slight curve across its width. This will make it easier to attach it to the lizard's body.

8 Tape the tail to the body. Use strips of sticky tape on top and underneath the tail to hold it securely in place.

Fix tape to the tube before attaching the tail.

Make the spikes
the same length as
the body and tail.

9 Lay the lizard on another piece of thin cardboard to *see* how big its **front legs** need to be. Draw the legs as a single piece. Repeat for the **back legs**.

10 Draw the lizard's **tongue** and **spikes** on a new piece of thin cardboard. Add a tab to the spikes. Then cut out all the body parts.

Add notches if
your lizard's tail
is curved so
you can bend
the spikes.

11 Flip the lizard over and attach the legs to the body with sticky tape. Make sure the toes are facing in the right direction.

12 Attach the spikes to the lizard's back. Fold the tab along the spikes first, to make the spikes stand upright. Then, starting at the tail end, tape the tab along the lizard's body and tail.

Add scales in a lighter
or darker shade.

Add a
tongue.

Paint the features
a different color
from the rest
of the body.

13 Your lizard is now ready to decorate. Paint it in bright colors and patterns. Don't forget to add the eyes.

NOW TRY THIS

If you've made several lizards, you probably need a place to put them on show. People who own real reptiles often keep them indoors in a special tank called a vivarium. Why not use a cardboard box to build a vivarium for your lizards? You could even decorate it with exotic plants, which you can make by following steps 3–8 of the Tropical Aquarium project on pages 70–71.

1 Take a medium-sized, shallow cardboard box and cut off the flaps. Do not discard them.

2 Position the flaps inside so they form a shelf and a ramp. Tape them securely in place.

3 Paint the inside of the box. Once the paint dries, your vivarium is ready for your lizards to move in.

Paint the ramp and shelf in a dark color to make the lizards stand out.

Arrange the plants and lizards until you are happy with the display.

Race your rabbits
toward the carrots.

RULES OF
THE GAME

• In this four-player game, the aim is to
be the first player to get your rabbit to
the carrots at the end of the racetrack.

• Throw a dice (or spin a spinner) and
move your rabbit forward according
to the number it shows.

• Go forward two more spaces if you
land on a pink line.

• Go back two spaces if you land
on an orange line.

• Go back to the start of the racetrack
if you land on another rabbit.

Decorate each
racetrack to look like a
vegetable patch.

Paper tubes support the rabbits on the racetrack.

RACING RABBITS

You'll love playing this thrilling rabbit race game! Make two vegetable patches with high fences for the rabbits to jump over. Then challenge your friends to see whose rabbit can get to the tasty carrots first.

Add fences to the racetracks.

This is the start of your racetrack.

HOW TO MAKE
RACING RABBITS

The first thing you'll need to make for this game is two identical cardboard racetracks. Measure both racetracks carefully so nobody has an unfair advantage when you play the game. Then use the template to make rabbits to race along the tracks.

Take your time to make sure everything is the right size and fits together.

Difficulty level:
Medium

YOU WILL NEED

Paints

Glue

Paintbrushes

Cardboard

Adhesive putty

Sticky tape

Pencil

Scissors

Paper

Ruler

Thin cardboard box

1 To make the **first racetrack**, draw a 8 x 24 in (20 x 60 cm) rectangle on cardboard. Add dotted lines 2 in (5 cm) in from the long edges.

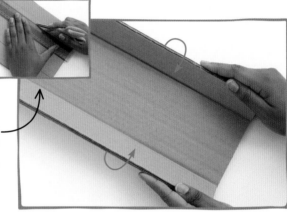

Fold upward to make the sides of the racetrack.

2 Cut the rectangle out. Score along the dotted lines and fold the sides upward.

Flatten the rectangle again before marking the edges.

3 Draw a line ½ in (1 cm) in from one long edge of the rectangle. Then draw lines 1 in (2 cm) apart to divide the edge into equally spaced sections. Repeat the process on the other side.

4 Use a ruler to draw a symmetrical triangle inside each of the smaller sections that you have drawn along the edges of the racetrack.

5 Cut out around the triangles to leave a zigzag edge. This will hold your rabbits in place. **Repeat steps 1–5 to make the second racetrack.**

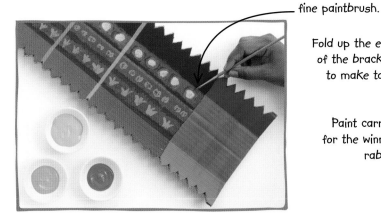

Paint on the details with a fine paintbrush.

6 Paint the racetracks and leave them to dry. Add pink and orange lines that reach from one side to the other.

Fold up the ends of the brackets to make tabs.

Paint carrots for the winning rabbit.

7 To make the **start** and **end brackets**, cut out four strips of cardboard that are about 2 in (5 cm) wider than the racetracks. Paint them brown, with carrot details on the two end brackets.

8 Fold the sides of the racetracks back up. Then glue the tabs on the brackets to the ends of each racetrack.

Your finished racetracks should be identical.

9 To make the **fenceposts**, draw a 7 x 20 cm (3 x 8 in) rectangle and divide it into eight equal sections. Mark a triangle on each post to match the notches on the racetrack and cut the fenceposts out.

10 Now make the **fences**. Draw four 2½ x 3½ in (6 x 9 cm) rectangles with ½ in (1 cm) tabs at either end.

11 Cut all four rectangles out, then score along the tabs and fold them up.

12 Paint your fences green, then add the fence details in white. Paint the fenceposts black and white.

13 Glue the fenceposts to the edge of the racetrack. Then glue the tabs of the fences to the fenceposts. Each racetrack should have two fences with a post on each side of the fence.

Copy the circle for the hole from the rabbit templates.

14 Now use the rabbit templates (page 135) to draw four **rabbits** on cardboard. Cut them out and paint them. Then pierce a hole in each rabbit using a pencil tip and carefully cut it out.

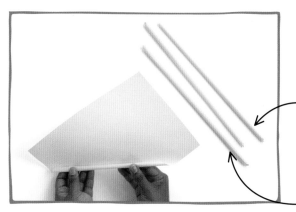

Make the tubes wide enough to fit snugly through the holes in the rabbits.

The tubes must be slightly longer than the width of the racetrack.

15 Roll four sheets of paper tightly into tubes and secure the edges with sticky tape. These will support your rabbits on the racetracks.

16 Paint the tubes in colors that match the backgrounds of your rabbit pieces. Then let the paint dry.

The rabbits can also land on the fenceposts.

17 Push and twist the tubes through the holes in the rabbits. Rest the rabbits on the notches of the racetracks, and trim the ends of the tubes if they are too long.

18 Now, challenge your friends to a rabbit race! See page 44 for the rules of the game.

NOW TRY THIS

If you prefer more exotic animals, why not make a kangaroo-themed racing game? You can also make a spinner to use instead of a dice.

Use the kangaroo template (page 135).

Use the spinner template (page 135).

Paint your racetrack in golden-brown colors.

Push a pencil through the middle.

PUPPET DRAGON

Dragons have appeared in myths and legends around the world for thousands of years. Now you can bring a flying dragon to life! Make it roar and snap its jaws with just a flick of your fingers.

HOW TO MAKE A
PUPPET DRAGON

This hand puppet uses six different templates, so make sure you will have enough cardboard. Remember that you will need two big wings so that your dragon can fly!

Turn to pages 136–137 to **check the templates** before you start.

Difficulty level: Medium

YOU WILL NEED

Paints

Scissors

Pencil

Paintbrushes

Glue

Thin cardboard box

Sticky tape

Cardboard sheets

1 Make the puppet's **upper jaw** first. Cut out a cardboard rectangle that's a little larger than your hand.

2 Fold the piece in the middle. Slide your fingers into the folded cardboard to make sure that they fit.

3 Tape both sides of the jaw piece together, keeping enough room for your fingers.

4 Repeat **steps 1–3** with a rectangle that is the same length, but half as wide. This will be the **lower jaw**, which will fit over your thumb.

Make sure the openings are in the middle.

5 To connect the jaws, cut out a strip of thin cardboard that is narrower than the lower jaw. Tape it to both jaw pieces.

6 Fold the jaw so that the connecting strip of cardboard is in the middle. Try on the completed jaw, with your thumb inside the lower jaw.

Tongue

Whisker

Fang

7 Copy the **whisker, tongue,** and **fang** templates (including tabs, where necessary) from pages 136–137 onto a piece of cardboard. You will need a pair of whiskers and two fangs.

8 Cut out the five pieces. Then, add tabs to the fangs and whiskers (but not the tongue) by folding each piece along the line at the base.

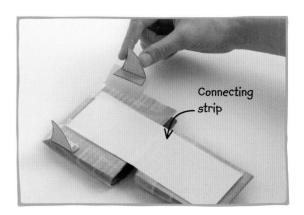

Connecting strip

9 Lay the jaw section flat with the connecting strip facing up, and attach the fangs by taping their tabs to either side of the upper jaw.

10 Flip the jaw section over and tape the tabs of the whiskers to the front corners of the upper jaw. Bend the whiskers into curves.

11 To complete the puppet's mouth, tape the straight edge of the tongue to the center of the front of the lower jaw, so the tip sticks out.

13 Tape the tab of the head section to the back of the dragon's upper jaw. Your puppet's head is now complete!

Tape the head so that it sits at the back of the jaw.

12 Copy the **head** template from page 136 onto some cardboard and cut it out. Fold along the base line to create a tab. Draw eyes above the tab.

The whiskers should curl out.

You can curl the tongue piece if you like.

The neck should be narrower than the width of the lower jaw.

14 Copy the **body and tail** template from page 137 onto some cardboard and cut it out.

15 Copy the **wing** template from page 136 onto a piece of cardboard and cut it out.

16 Repeat **step** 15 for the second wing, and flip it over so you have a symmetrical pair of wings. Tape them together as shown.

17 Tape the body section you made in **step** 14 centrally across the wings, as shown. Turn it over and tape the other side if it doesn't feel secure.

18 It's time to paint your puppet. Start with the head section. Paint it in a *base* color first, let it dry, then paint the details on.

19 While the head section dries, decorate the puppet's body on both sides. Use bright colors to make your dragon bold and impressive. Let all the paint on the body section dry.

20 It's time to attach the body to the head. Dab glue along the edge of the neck.

Open and close the mouth by using your hand.

21 Flip the body over and stick the neck to the underside of the lower jaw. Let the glue dry.

22 Now you can try your puppet on properly. Put your hand inside as shown, with the body hanging in front of your arm.

NOW TRY THIS

Now that you know how to make a puppet dragon, you can create other equally fabulous creatures with only a few changes. **Repeat steps 1–3** from the dragon, then make the alterations described below.

PUPPET FROG

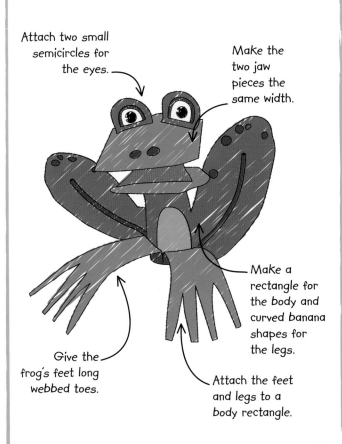

Attach two small semicircles for the eyes.

Make the two jaw pieces the same width.

Give the frog's feet long webbed toes.

Make a rectangle for the body and curved banana shapes for the legs.

Attach the feet and legs to a body rectangle.

PUPPET BIRD

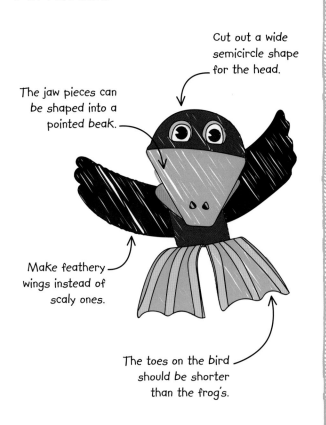

Cut out a wide semicircle shape for the head.

The jaw pieces can be shaped into a pointed beak.

Make feathery wings instead of scaly ones.

The toes on the bird should be shorter than the frog's.

HERO'S HELMET

No knight would be ready for battle without a helmet. Make your own protective headgear, complete with a visor, faceguard, and feather plume. Or, if knights are too old-fashioned, whip up a superhero mask or racing helmet.

HOW TO MAKE A
HERO'S HELMET

This knight's helmet looks impressive but it's not hard to make. You can either ask someone to help you build it around your head, or make a balloon stand (see page 12) to give you a sturdy structure to work around. If you want to be sure that it will fit, you can measure each strip of cardboard against your head before you cut it.

> Make sure the balloon stand is **the right size**. You want a helmet that fits!
>
> **Difficulty level:** Medium

YOU WILL NEED

Paints

Strong tape

Paintbrushes

Scissors

Pencil

Cardboard sheets

1 To make the **frame**, cut out two long strips of cardboard. Wrap one horizontally around your balloon stand at mouth height. Bend the other strip over the top, angling it toward the back slightly.

2 Stick the two strips together on either side of the join, using strong tape. Repeat on the other side.

3 Now bring the ends of the horizontal strip together, at the front of the balloon stand. Overlap the edges slightly and tape them together.

4 Trim the ends off the vertical strip, so they are level with the horizontal strip. Add extra tape on the inside to strengthen the joins.

5 To fill in the hole at the back of the helmet, cut out three cardboard rectangles. Position one of your rectangles centrally and secure it with strong tape.

Tape each piece top and bottom.

6 Tape the other two rectangles on either side of the piece you attached in **step 5**, to cover the gaps.

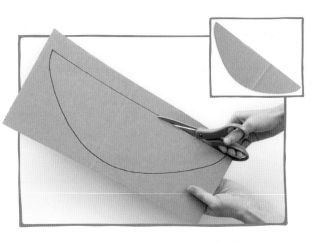

Bend the pieces to the curve of the helmet.

7 To make the **visor**, draw a stretched semicircle shape on a piece of cardboard and then cut the shape out.

Tape the visor in an "open" position so that it won't cover your eyes.

8 Bend the visor into a curved shape and tape the ends to either side of your helmet. Tape it on the inside too, to strengthen it.

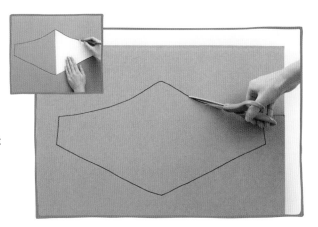

9 Use the template on page 138 to draw half of the **faceguard** on a piece of cardboard. Flip the template to draw the other half, then cut it out.

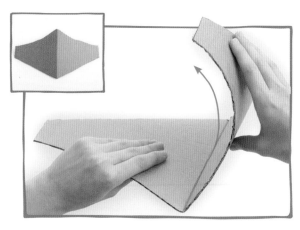

10 Fold the faceguard in half from point to point, then *bend* it into a curved shape on either side of the fold.

11 With the folded edge pointing outward, attach the ends of the faceguard to either side of the helmet, using strong tape.

12 Now make the **plume**. Lay your helmet on its side on a piece of cardboard and use it as a guide to draw the plume. Then cut out the shape.

Make two tabs the same size.

Tape the pieces to the plume first.

13 To attach the plume to the helmet, cut out two cardboard rectangles. Fold the pieces in half to create tabs, then tape them to the plume.

14 Position the plume against the *back* of the helmet and tape the tabs down.

15 Your Knight's helmet is now ready to decorate. Use gray or silver paint to create a metal effect. Paint the plume in any color you want.

Swirls of paint make a good feather pattern.

Add joints and bolts to make the helmet look realistic.

NOW TRY THIS

You can use the basic frame of the knight's helmet to make other types of headgear. How about a crash helmet to go with the race car on page 108, or a superhero's mask? Simply repeat **steps 1-6** to create the frame and then add different features.

Wide visor

Streamlining stripes

V-shaped visor

Nose piece

To make a **racing helmet**, make a wide visor which covers more of your face. Then you are ready to race!

For a **superhero's mask**, make the visor a V-shape and position it lower. Cut out a gap for your mouth and add a nose piece.

Bottle tops and buttons make great robot features.

BOX ROBOTS

Would you like to travel through time to the distant future? Now you can, by transforming yourself into an incredible sci-fi robot! You'll need cardboard boxes that you can wear on your head, body, and hands. Then bring your box robot to life with mechanical designs.

Paint high-tech designs onto all parts of your box robot.

HOW TO MAKE
BOX ROBOTS

To make this fantastic robot costume, you'll need a big box for the robot's body, a square box for its head, and two smaller boxes for its hands. Make sure the boxes are big enough for you to wear. You'll be using cardboard circles and cups to add the robot's ears and eyes.

Take your time when you cut holes in the boxes for **a perfect fit**.

Difficulty level:
Medium

YOU WILL NEED

Ruler

Paper cups

Large plate

Scissors

Strong tape   Pencil   Paintbrushes

Paints

Cardboard boxes

You'll need cardboard sheets, a large box for the body, a smaller square box for the head, and two small boxes for the hands.

Mark the position of your eyes with two dots.

1 Place the square box over your head and mark the position of your eyes. Then remove the box and draw around the dots. Cut this shape out to make a slot for you to see through.

Use a ruler to draw your cross.

2 To create the **ears**, trace around a large plate on a piece of card. Mark the center of the circle with a cross, then cut the circle out.

3 Cut along one arm of the cross from the outside of the circle to the center. Cut short slits across the other arms of the cross and fold them upward to make tabs.

Keep the tabs at the center folded over.

Fix the ears to the robot's head.

4 Pull the circle into a cone shape. Secure the overlapping edges of the cone with strong tape. **Repeat steps 2–4** to make a second ear.

5 To attach the ears, tape the tabs at the center of each cone to the sides of the box.

Cut slightly above the bottom of the cups.

6 Now, make the **eyes**. Cut the base off two paper cups. Make slits around the bottom of each cup to create tabs.

7 Fold the tabs outward so that you can easily stick the eyes to the robot's head.

8 Stick the eyes to the head by taping the tabs down.

Look at the position of the ears and attach the eyes at a similar height.

Your antenna can be any shape and size.

9 Draw an **antenna** shape on cardboard. You can use the picture above as a guide if you like. Cut the shape out.

11 Tape the support in place on top of the robot's head, then tape the antenna to the support.

Tape the longer flap to the head, and the antenna to the shorter flap.

13 Use a large plate to draw circles on the other two sides of the box. Cut the circles out to make holes for your arms.

10 Make a **support** for the robot antenna. Cut out a small rectangle with tabs on two of the sides as shown, and fold the tabs up.

Make the shape wide enough to fit your head through.

12 Now make the robot's **body**. Cut off one of the sides of the large box. Then draw a U shape on the opposite side and cut it out.

Make sure your pieces of cardboard are wider than your small boxes.

14 Next, make the robot's **hands**. Cut out two rectangular pieces of cardboard, roll them into tubes, and secure them with strong tape.

15 Take one of the small boxes and draw around the tube on each shorter side near the bottom. Then cut holes where you have drawn.

16 Push a tube through the two holes to make handles you can hold when you wear them.
Repeat steps 15 and 16 to make the other hand.

17 Finally, decorate each part of your robot. Paint a base coat first and let it dry. Then paint on futuristic designs in bright colors.

Make your decorations look like buttons, dials, screens, and switches.

Paint the head and ears in contrasting colors.

NOW TRY THIS

Why not make your robot even more high-tech by adding three-dimensional features to it? Try sticking on plastic lids, parts of egg cartons, and other cardboard shapes.

Egg carton dividers

Plastic lids

Give your robot big eyes using plastic lids.

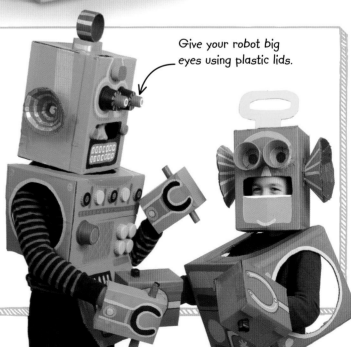

TROPICAL AQUARIUM

Keeping an aquarium is a popular hobby for people around the world. Now you can make your own underwater scene, complete with colorful fish. All careful aquarists (people who keep aquariums) make sure their fish live in an environment similar to their natural habitats. So make a variety of coral, rocks, and underwater plants for your fish to hide among.

TROPICAL AQUARIUM

Turn your cardboard box into a beautiful aquarium with lots of coral features. Then, use the templates on page 139 to make a colorful array of tropical fish to display inside your aquatic world.

The **more features** you add to your aquarium, the more impressive it will look!

Difficulty level: Medium

YOU WILL NEED

Paper

Cardboard sheets

Cardboard box with flaps removed

Thin cardboard box

Pencil

Egg carton

Paints

Paintbrushes

String

Scissors

Wooden sticks

Sticky tape

Ruler

1 First, make your **tank**. Paint the inside of your box dark blue. Paint the base in light blue and use the same light blue color to paint wavy lines for a watery effect.

2 While the tank dries, make the various coral features. First, cut off the lid of your egg carton to use as the **table coral**.

3 Carefully use your scissors to cut around the two central dividers inside your egg carton, to make **cone-shaped corals**.

4 To make an **ocean plant**, cut a rectangle out of thin cardboard. Then cut wavy slits across it, leaving a 1 in (2 cm) edge for the base.

5 Roll up the piece of cardboard tightly, starting from the base, so it forms a thin tube.

6 Then, hold the base so it remains rolled up, and wrap a piece of sticky tape around it to secure.

7 Bend the strips outward to form the plant shape. Repeat **steps 4–7** to make plants of different shapes and sizes.

Hold and push the base on so you don't damage the plant.

8 Next, use a pencil to pierce the tops of your coral cones and push the base of a plant into each one.

9 Now turn your egg carton over and cut out the two remaining pieces at the end of your box, to make a double **dome-shaped coral**.

10 Take your double dome-shaped corals and pierce the tops in the same way as **step 8**. Push some more plants into the holes.

11 To make a **coral panel**, tear off a piece of corrugated cardboard. Carefully peel away the thin top layer to revel the bumpy texture underneath.

12 Use a ruler and scissors to score along the length of the panel, about 1 in (2 cm) from the base. Repeat **steps 11–12** to make more coral panels.

Use lighter colors
to add detail to
your plants.

Use contrasting colors
to add detail and
texture to your coral.

Paint your table
coral all one color.

Corrugated cardboard
gives a nice texture to
coral panels.

Use paper to
make rocks.

13 Paint your coral features in bright colors. Add **rocks** to your scene by scrunching up paper into balls and paint them, too.

14 Once your painted pieces are dry, add a strip of sticky tape along the base of your **coral panels.**

15 Then, stick them inside your aquarium. Place one on the bottom and stick another to the side.

16 Now, arrange the rest of your coral features and rocks inside the aquarium however you want.

17 To make **tropical fish**, use the templates on page 139 to draw fish on thin cardboard, then cut them out.

18 Paint your collection of fish in bold colors and pretty patterns, adding eyes, mouths, and gills.

19 To add your beautiful fish to the aquarium, tape a piece of string to the back of a few of your fish.

20 Then, use a sharp pencil to carefully pierce holes at the top of your aquarium.

21 Feed each piece of string through a hole from the inside and secure it with a knot.

22 Finally, tape the remaining fish to wooden sticks and push the ends into the coral shelf and features to complete the scene.

Adjust the strings so that the fish are hanging at different heights.

Paint the wooden sticks blue so they match the ocean scene.

NOW TRY THIS

To add some movement to your underwater scene, carefully cut thin slots out of the sides of your aquarium. Then draw two of your favorite sea creatures on thin cardboard. Cut them out and decorate them, then tape each one to a long wooden stick. Poke your new sea creatures through the slots of your aquarium, to create your own aquatic show!

Use painted wooden sticks to move your sea creatures.

Cut a narrow opening along each side of the aquarium.

PHARAOH'S FINERY

Make your own Egyptian headdress, fit for a pharaoh and perfect for any fancy dress occasion.

Scarab beetle decoration

Add a collar to make your outfit even more impressive.

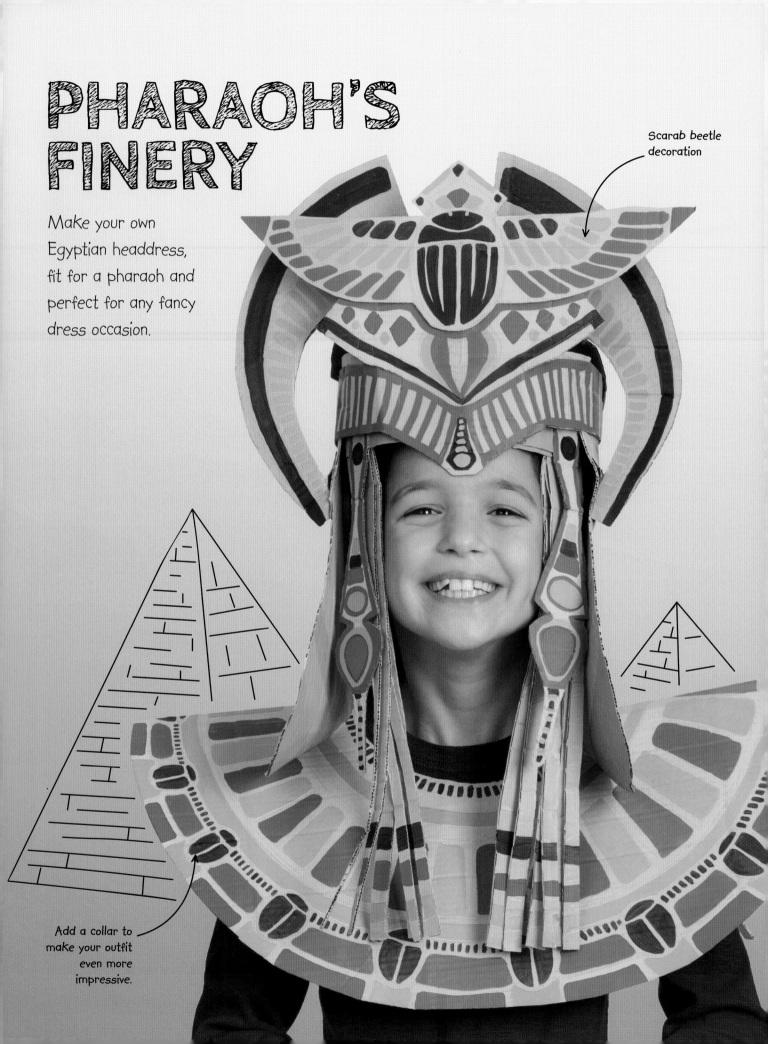

HOW TO MAKE
PHARAOH'S FINERY

You'll look fabulous in this dazzling Egyptian headdress!
Take your time and decorate it however you want,
but make sure you choose nice bright colors. It is
important to measure each piece against your body
and adjust the size to fit you, so you may want to
ask someone to help.

Copy your
templates really
carefully for
this project.

Difficulty level:
Medium

YOU WILL NEED

Pencil

Paintbrushes

Double-sided tape

Strong tape

Cardboard sheets

Scissors

Paints

Ruler

1 Cut a strip of cardboard and wrap it around
your head for a snug fit. Trim off any excess,
then tape the ends together to make a **headband**.

2 To make the **frontpiece**,
cut a piece of cardboard that is slightly
wider than the headband and half its length.
Fold the piece in half, draw a curved line along
the bottom, and cut along the line.

The tip should
be at the front
of the headband.

3 Tape the frontpiece
to the headband.
The tip of the frontpiece
should sit in the center
of your forehead.

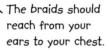

The braids should reach from your ears to your chest.

4 Next, make the **braids.** Cut out two identical rectangles of cardboard, and use a ruler to draw straight lines across them. Cut along the lines, but don't cut all the way to the end.

5 Paint the braids a yellow base coat. Then add details to the tips in contrasting colors.

If you like, you can copy the details from the pendant template.

6 Now make the **pendants**. Use the pendant template on page 140 to draw two shapes on cardboard. Cut the pendant shapes out.

7 Paint a yellow base coat on the pendants and add details in contrasting colors once the paint has dried.

Tip of the frontpiece

Tape the braids to the inside of the headband.

8 Once the braids are dry, tape them to the inside of the headband on either side, so they will dangle over your ears.

You can paint over the tape when you paint the headband.

9 Once the pendants are dry, use strong tape to attach them to the outside of the headband so they hang over the braids.

Cut along your markings to around the ends of the strip.

10 To make the **hood**, cut a strip of cardboard long enough to reach from one collarbone to the other when curved over your head. Draw around a roll of tape at each end.

11 Bend the hood into a curved shape so that it will fit snugly over the top of your head when you attach it to the headband.

Flip the template over to draw the second half of the *scarab beetle.*

12 Use strong tape to secure the hood to the headband. Place the hood over the braids, but make sure it doesn't cover the pendants.

13 Next, use the scarab beetle template on page 140 to draw half of the **scarab beetle**. Flip it over to draw the other side, then cut the scarab out.

15 Carefully stick the scarab beetle to the top of the frontpiece. Its bottom point should line up with the tip.

Press down firmly at the front to attach the scarab beetle in place.

14 Draw scarab details onto the shape in pencil. You can copy the details from the template. Then put double-sided tape on the back of the shape, along the bottom.

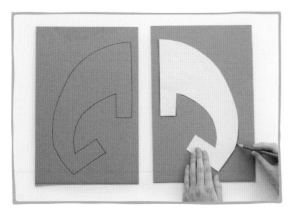

16 Use the template on page 141 to draw the first **crown piece** on cardboard. Flip the template to draw the second one. Cut both pieces out.

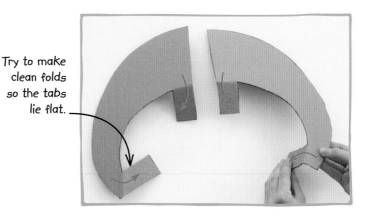

Try to make clean folds so the tabs lie flat.

17 Fold the tabs on the crown pieces back on themselves, as shown above. This will help you secure the crown pieces to the hood.

18 Attach the tabs of the crown pieces to the top of the hood using strong tape.

Use a fine paintbrush to carefully paint the details on the scarab beetle.

Paint both sides of the hood.

19 It's time to decorate your headdress. Paint the headband and hood a base color first, and then add patterns in other colors once the paint has dried.

NOW TRY THIS

Make some matching accessories to complete your pharaoh outfit. For the **cuffs**, you will need two strips of cardboard long enough to wrap around your wrist, with some excess. For the **collar**, you will need a large piece of cardboard wider than your shoulders.

HOW TO MAKE CUFFS

Mark where the cuff fits around your wrist.

1 Cut a slit near one end of your cardboard strip. Wrap the strip tightly around your wrist, and slot the other end through the slit.

Edges can be curved.

2 Cut along the mark for the second slit and trim off excess cardboard. Now make a second cuff.

3 Paint the cuffs one color and let them dry. Then draw details in pencil and paint them in contrasting colors to match the headdress.

HOW TO MAKE A COLLAR

1 Cut out a large oval piece of cardboard. Then use a plate to draw a circle that will make a hole wide enough for your neck to fit through.

2 Cut out the shape, with an opening between the inner circle and outer oval so that you can put the collar on.

3 Bend the front and back of the piece so that the collar curves over your shoulders when you wear it.

4 Paint the piece all one color and leave it to dry. Draw the details in pencil and paint them in striking colors.

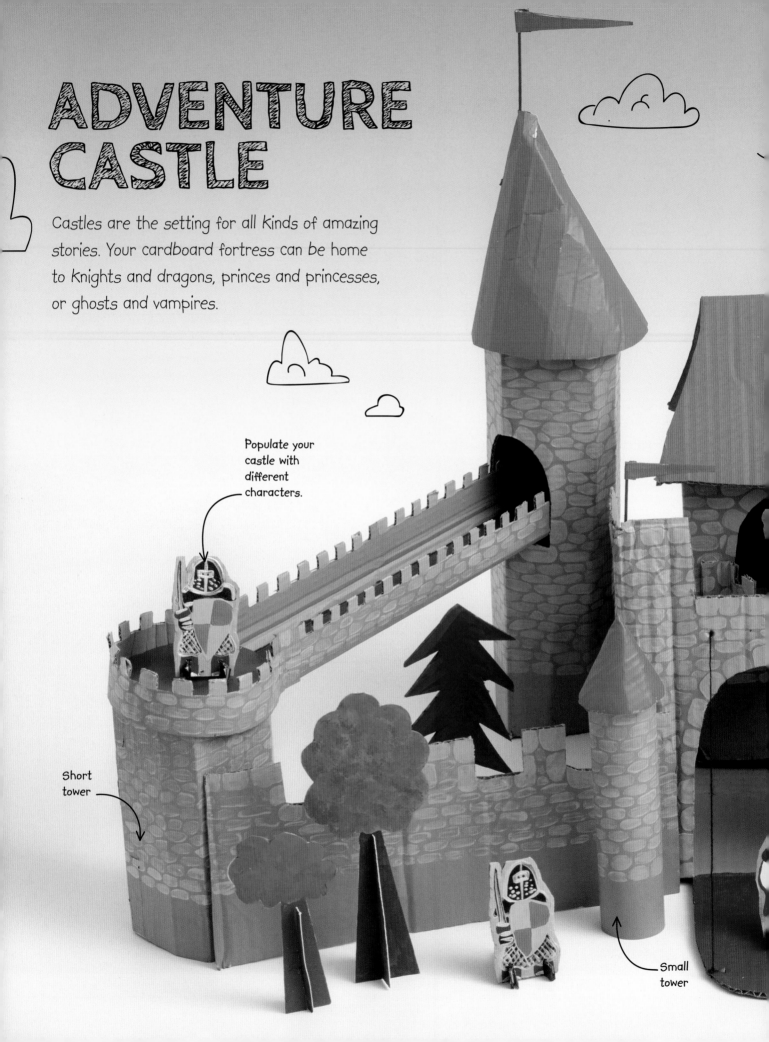

ADVENTURE CASTLE

Castles are the setting for all kinds of amazing stories. Your cardboard fortress can be home to knights and dragons, princes and princesses, or ghosts and vampires.

Populate your castle with different characters.

Short tower

Small tower

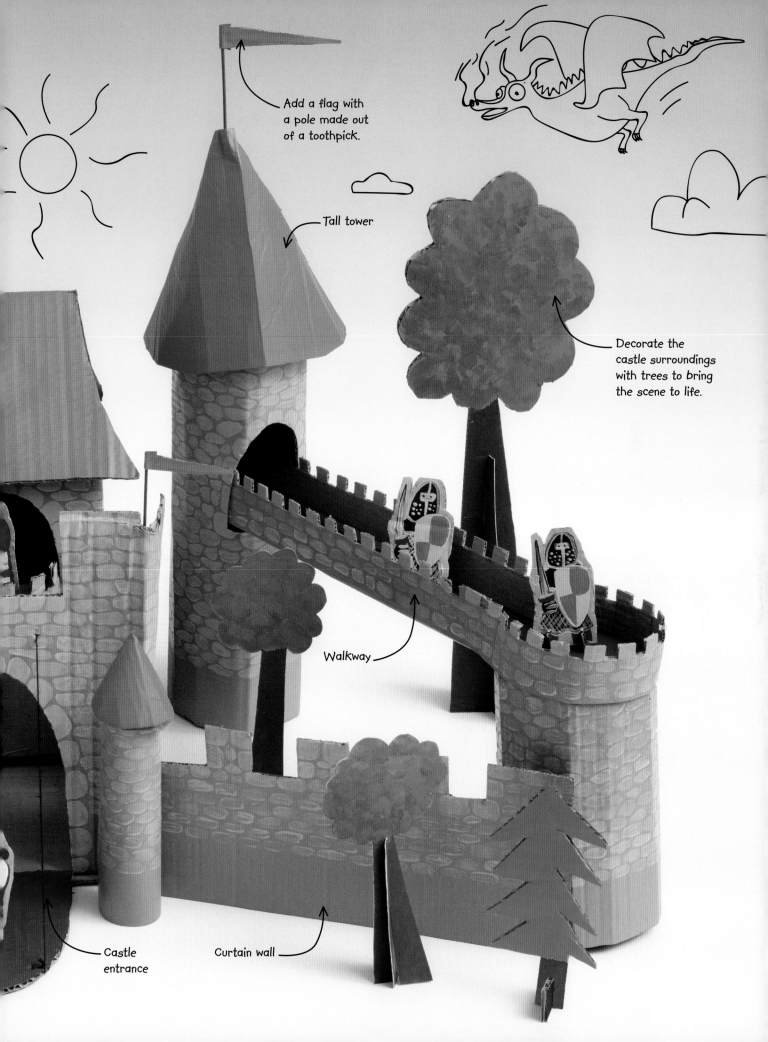

Add a flag with a pole made out of a toothpick.

Tall tower

Decorate the castle surroundings with trees to bring the scene to life.

Walkway

Castle entrance

Curtain wall

HOW TO MAKE AN
ADVENTURE CASTLE

The main part of the castle is made out of a large cardboard box. Keep the bits you cut off and use them to make the walkways and towers.

You'll need **plenty of space** for building this large model!

Difficulty level:
Medium

YOU WILL NEED

Ruler

Paintbrushes

Thread

Strong tape

Scissors

Pencil

Glue

Paints

Cardboard boxes

Cardboard sheets

1 Make the **entrance** out of your large box. On the front, draw a rectangle for the **roof** and the **drawbridge** below.

2 Draw a **staircase** on one side. Extend the line from the lowest step across the back wall. Add a **window** below the stairs.

3 Cut out the drawbridge, leaving it attached at the base, and fold it out. Cut out the rectangular piece at the top.

4 Carefully cut out the window and staircase. Keep the pieces that you cut out so you can trace around them.

5 Trace around the pieces you cut in **step 4** to draw a window and staircase on the other side of the box.

6 Cut out the window and staircase on the other side. Cut off the back wall along the line you marked in **step 2**.

7 To complete the drawbridge, pierce two holes into the top of the drawbridge and two holes in the wall above.

8 Cut a long piece of thread. Feed it through the four holes and tie the ends together.

Cut a rectangle large enough to create a pitched roof for your keep.

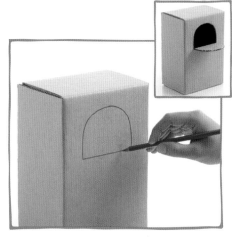

9 Make the **keep** out of your small box. Draw a **window** on the front. Cut it out, leaving it attached at the base, and fold it outward.

10 For the **roof**, draw a rectangle with a line through the center and tab outlines at each end. Cut the roof out.

11 Fold the roof along the central line. Fold the tabs inward and glue them to the top of the keep.

Battlements
are the notches
along the top of
castle walls.

12 Draw **battlements** on a cardboard strip with tabs at either end. Cut the strip out, fold the tabs over, and tape the tabs to the keep so the strip fits around the window ledge.

13 Now make a **short tower**. Cut out a piece of cardboard 14 in (35 cm) long and as tall as the castle entrance. Roll it into a tube.

14 Bring the ends together so they overlap by 2 in (5 cm) and tape the edge down. Repeat **steps** 13 and 14 to create another short tower.

15 To add **flat roofs** to your short towers, draw around the towers on a piece of cardboard.

The end you
draw around will
become the top
of the tower.

Fix tape on
the outside.

16 Cut out the two circular shapes and tape them to the top of the towers. All that remains is adding **battlements** to the towers.

17 To make the battlements, draw a 12 x 3 in (30 x 8 cm) rectangle. Add a line across the center and a row of small squares along the edges.

18 Cut the piece along the horizontal line to make two identical pieces. Then, cut out every other square tab to complete the battlements.

Do not tape the battlements all the way around the short tower.

19 Wrap a battlement strip around the top of each short tower. Tape the middle section to the tower and leave the ends loose.

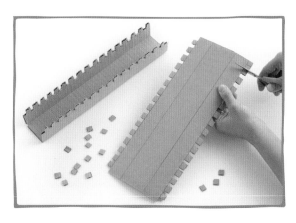

20 For the **walkway**, cut out a 12 x 5 in (30 x 12 cm) cardboard piece. Cut battlements into the sides. Score and fold the piece 1½ in (4 cm) from each edge.

21 Tape the walkway to the ends of the battlements strip you wrapped around the first tower. Repeat **steps** 20 and 21 to add a walkway to the other short tower.

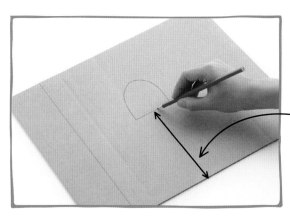

Height of short tower.

22 Make a **tall tower** out of a 12 x 14 in (30 x 36 cm) cardboard piece. Draw the **entrance**, making its base level with the height of the short tower.

23 Cut out the entrance. Roll the piece into a tube and tape the overlapping ends together. Repeat **steps** 22 and 23 to make another tall tower.

Add more tape to make the join stronger.

Push the roofs down onto the tall towers to the secure them in place.

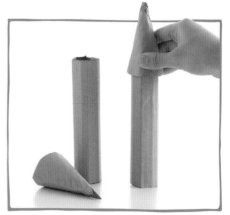

24 For the tower **roofs**, roll a 9 x 9 in (24 x 24 cm) cardboard piece diagonally into a cone and tape the ends together. Repeat to make another roof.

25 Hold each cone by the pointy end and trim the base to make it level all the way around.

26 Place the cone roofs on top of your tall towers. You do not need to tape them to the towers because they will stay in place when you push them down.

27 Link each short tower to a tall one by slotting the walkway into the tall tower entrance.

28 Make **small towers** out of cardboard pieces half the size of those used for the tall towers.

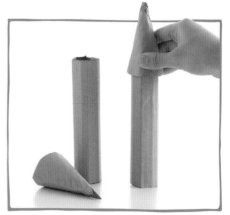

29 Repeat **steps 22–26** (without windows) to complete the small towers. They will flank the castle entrance.

30 Draw a **curtain wall** with battlements on cardboard and cut it out. Draw around it to make a second wall and cut it out.

Position the keep behind the castle entrance.

31 Now put the parts of the castle together. Finally, paint it in your chosen colors. You may want to paint the walls in a *base* color first and then paint on the stony effect.

NOW TRY THIS

Populate your castle with an array of characters. Draw their outlines on cardboard (or use the templates on page 139), cut them out, and paint on the faces and bodies. To make a stand, cut two slits at the base of each character and push the ends of a folded strip of cardboard into the slits.

The stand is made out of a folded strip of cardboard.

Your characters can be good, evil, magical, historical, or spooky. You decide!

PENGUIN FAMILY

If you've ever enjoyed watching penguins splashing around at the zoo, you'll love playing with these adorable creatures! All you need to make them is a sheet of cardboard. Penguins are extremely sociable animals, so why not make an entire family of penguins to keep each other company?

HOW TO MAKE A
PENGUIN FAMILY

To make this family of friendly penguins, you'll need to follow the penguin template (page 142) very carefully. Don't cut the strips in your cardboard too far, and make sure you always know which part of the penguin each strip will be.

Make sure you **slot your strips of cardboard** into the right place.

Difficulty level:
Medium

YOU WILL NEED

Thin cardboard box

Paints

Scissors

Sticky tape

Paintbrushes

Pencil

Ruler

1 Cut out a large piece of thin cardboard. Then copy the penguin template on page 142 onto your cardboard. Use a ruler to keep your lines straight.

2 Cut slits along the lines. You should have seven strips to make various parts of the penguin, plus a thin strip at either end for the stand.

3 Carefully copy the words on the template to label each strip with the correct part of the penguin. Look at the picture above to help you.

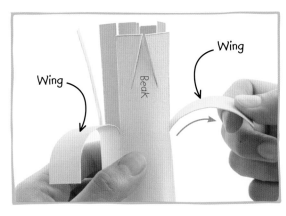

Tape along the inside of the tube to secure it.

Wing

Wing

Beak

4 To make the penguin's **body**, roll the cardboard into a tube so that the two strips at the end for the stand overlap. Then secure the base with sticky tape.

5 Make the penguin's **wings**. Gently bend the wing strips outward to give your penguin a pair of flapping wings.

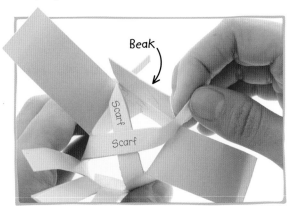

Beak

Scarf

Scarf

7 Look at your penguin in progress. Make sure you are clear which strip is which.

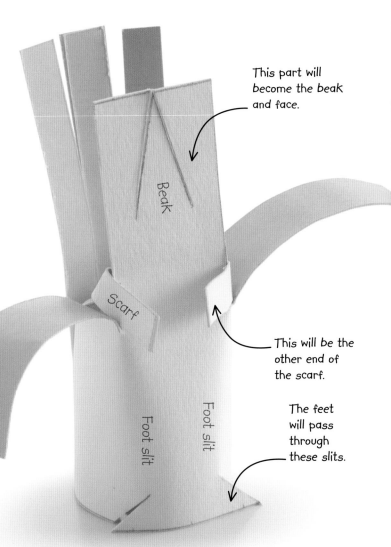

This part will become the beak and face.

Beak

Scarf

This will be the other end of the scarf.

The feet will pass through these slits.

Foot slit

Foot slit

6 Create the **scarf** by bending the scarf strips inwards so they cross inside the tube. Slot the ends on either side of the beak strip at the front.

8 Bend the **beak** section back slightly and wrap the scarf strips around the base. Draw a short line where the strips meet in the middle, as shown.

Lock the strips
in place using
the slits.

Don't cut any
farther than
your pencil
marks.

Wing

9 Cut slits along the pencil marks in the scarf strips. Make sure you don't cut all the way through the strips.

10 Pull the strips back into position and fasten them together by slotting the slits into one another to secure the scarf.

11 Now make the **feet.** Bend the two foot strips outward and pull them back underneath the tube. Then turn your penguin around.

12 Bring the foot strips to the front of the penguin and slot them into the foot slits. Fold down the ends of the strips to create **toes.**

If the feet slide out of
place, secure them from
the inside with sticky tape.

13 Now make the penguin's **face.** Fold the V shape in the beak strip outward to make the **beak.** Then, bend the tops of the two strips on either side of the beak into curved **eye** shapes.

14 Finally, bend the remaining strip at the back of the penguin into an arc shape. You can use this strip to stand your penguin up.

15 Check that the strips are in the right place before you paint your penguin.

The strip at the back should prop your penguin up.

16 Now decorate your penguin. Use a fun, bright color for the scarf.

Paint eyes on these flaps.

Paint the penguin's body black and white, and its beak and feet orange.

Paint both sides of each foot.

Make each tube the same color as the penguin's scarf.

NOW TRY THIS

Turn your penguins into players for an icy-themed version of the game Racing Rabbits, featured on page 44. Follow the instructions on pages 46–49 to make the racecourses and paint them to look like icy streams. Use a sharp pencil to pierce a hole through the penguin's body just below the wings. Then push a colored tube through the hole.

CARDVILLE CITY

Welcome to Cardville, a city where everything is made from recycling! By gathering up boxes and tubes of all sizes, you can create any town you like, from a classic country village to a futuristic metropolis.

You can add extra tubes and triangles to make your buildings more elaborate.

Stack up tubes and boxes to create impressive skyscrapers.

HOW TO BUILD

CARDVILLE CITY

Cardville works best with lots of buildings, so make as many as you can. The good news is that they don't all need to be the same. Your city will look more realistic if your buildings are slightly different shapes and sizes.

Find all kinds of **small boxes and tubes** around the house, or make your own.

Difficulty level:
Hard

YOU WILL NEED

Thin cardboard box

Cardboard sheets

Small boxes and cardboard tubes

Sticky tape

Scissors

Pencil

Glue

Paintbrushes

Paints

BUILDINGS

1 If you can't find any small boxes for **buildings**, make your own. First, cut out a rectangle of thick cardboard. Fold it as shown to form a rectangular tube and secure it with sticky tape.

2 To make a **roof**, cut out a cardboard rectangle and fold it in half. Cut out two strips of thin cardboard and tape each one to either side of the fold. Then fold each thin piece of cardboard to create tabs.

3 To fix the roof in place, attach a piece of sticky tape to the end of each tab. Push each tab inside the tube and press the tape down against the walls.

4 Draw a **door** on the front of the building, then cut along one side and across the top. Fold the door outward to open it.

5 Repeat steps 1–4 as many times as you like to create houses of different shapes and sizes.

If you've made your own box, tape cardboard over the top.

7 Paint your buildings in a range of colors, adding windows and any other details you like.

Try picking out roofs and doors with bright colors.

6 Make **skyscrapers** by stacking up boxes and tubes of different sizes and attaching them together with glue or tape.

WALKWAY

Cut an X across the outline, then push the flaps into the box.

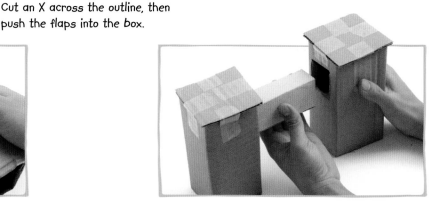

1 To make a **walkway**, take a long, thin box (or make your own box), line it up against the side of a building and draw around it. Cut across the outline and shape the flaps with your fingers to leave a neat hole.

2 Repeat the process with another similar building, then slot the ends of your walkway into the two holes. Tape in place if necessary.

CLOCK TOWER

Use a rectangle of thin cardboard to make the roof.

1 To make a **clock tower**, tape a short, wide box to the top of a tall, thin box. Add a roof as you did for the other buildings.

2 Stick a cardboard circle to the front of the smaller box. Then decorate your clock.

CITYSCAPE

Score lines across the road so it folds down neatly.

1 To build a **bridge**, take two small boxes and tape them to a strip of thick cardboard. Decorate the cardboard as a road and the boxes as brick walls.

2 To make a **garden hedge**, cut a strip of cardboard and fold it into a large square as shown. Tape the ends of the strip together.

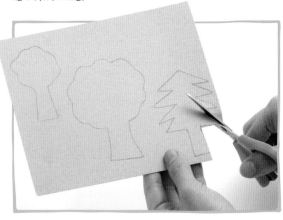

Use two different shades of green to give your plants a leafy texture.

3 To make **garden plants**, draw a variety of different trees and plants on a piece of thin cardboard and cut them out.

4 Glue the plants to the hedge, then decorate them with green and brown paint. Place a small house in the middle of your garden.

Cut slits in
the middle
of each wheel.

5 Draw a selection of different **cars** on thin cardboard and cut them out. Use scissors to snip small slits in the car wheels.

6 Cut out small rectangles of cardboard and snip short slits into them. Push them onto the wheels so that your cars can stand up.

Use a ruler
to draw
straight roads.

7 Paint your cars in nice bright colors, then add windows, dark-colored tires, and any other details you like, such as lights and bumpers.

8 Now plan out your city outline on a large sheet of thick cardboard. Sketch out roads, rivers, and landmarks in pencil.

9 Decorate your city outline, painting in the features you sketched in **step 8**. Add green painted boxes to vary the terrain. Then arrange your cars and buildings to create a bustling scene.

Arrange your walkway
so that it crosses
over the road.

DOME DEN

Have hours of fun playing outdoors or just relax and hide away in this special dome-shaped den. Once you've built your den, you can be as creative as you like when you decorate it. Paint the tiles in bold colors to make striking patterns, or even turn your den into a space base, woodland hideout, or igloo!

HOW TO MAKE A
DOME DEN

You'll be making almost 50 cardboard tiles for this dome den. Use your tile templates and make sure you measure your pieces really carefully, so that they fit together properly when you build your dome. You'll need strong tape to stick the tiles together, and lots of paint to decorate your finished dome.

> You'll need a lot of cardboard, and a **spare pair of hands** to help!
>
> Difficulty level: Hard

YOU WILL NEED

Cardboard sheets

Ruler

Scissors

Pencil

Strong tape

Paintbrushes

Paints

1 Lay your **triangle 1** template from page 142 on cardboard. Extend side A to 12¼ in (31 cm) and side B to 10¾ in (27.3 cm). Add a third line to complete the triangle, and cut the piece out.

B = 10¾ in

A = 12¼ in

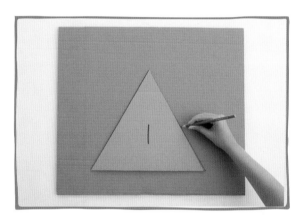

2 Lay the triangle on cardboard and draw around it to make an identical triangle.

3 Make a 1½ in (4 cm) cardboard strip and draw around it to add 1½ in (4 cm) tab outlines to all three sides of the triangle.

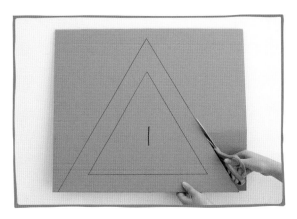

4 Cut out around the tab outlines of the triangle. This triangle will be used for your first **triangle 1 tile**.

5 Use your triangle 1 template to mark a straight line across the corners of the triangle. Cut along these lines. **Repeat steps 2-5 to make 30 triangle 1 tiles.**

A = 12¼ in
A = 12¼ in
A = 12¼ in

6 Now, lay the **triangle 2** template from page 143 on cardboard. Extend both sides to 12¼ in (31 cm) and join them up. Then, cut out the triangle and use it to **repeat step 2**.

7 Use the cardboard strip from **step 3** to add tabs to the triangle, then cut off the corners. **Repeat steps 6-7 to make nine triangle 2 tiles.**

12¼ in

8 To make your **square tiles**, draw a square on cardboard with lines that are 12¼ in (31 cm) long.

You will need to cut off the bottom tab.

9 Use the strip from **step 3** to add tabs to the square. Use the triangle 1 template to mark and cut the corners. Then cut off the bottom tab. **Repeat steps 8-9 to make nine square tiles.**

Line up the shorter "B" sides together.

10 Score along the tab lines of all three sets of tiles. Then fold along the score lines to finish making the tabs.

11 Arrange **five triangle 1 tiles** into a pentagon shape, so the tabs on the shorter sides meet. Use strong tape to fix the first two together.

Tape along the top and side of the tabs.

12 Secure the other edges in the same way. Then **repeat step 11** to make five more pentagons out of the remaining 25 triangle 1 tiles.

13 Now lay two pentagons next to each other, as shown, and slot a **triangle 2 tile** in between them. Tape the tabs to connect the triangle to the pentagons.

Connect your pentagons to make a single long curve.

14 **Repeat step 13** to attach three more pentagons to the two you've already connected. Once finished, you will have a single, long curving piece. This is the **roof section**!

Keep the sixth pentagon for the top of your dome.

16 Slot the **five remaining triangle 2 tiles** into the V-shaped spaces around the dome's top edge. Line up the tabs and tape them together.

15 Stand the whole piece up and pull the ends towards each other to form a circular shape. Leave a gap at the front for the top of the door, so you can easily enter the den.

17 Place the remaining pentagon into the gap at the **top of your dome**. Tape the tabs together to complete the roof of the dome.

18 Now, make the **wall of your dome**. Start by taping the left-hand tab of one **square tile** to the right-hand tab of another square tile.

Ensure the remaining tabs are at the top.

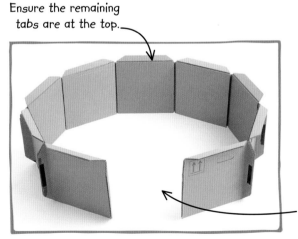

19 Repeat step 18 to link all nine square tiles in a line. Stand the piece up and arrange it into a circle. You have now finished the wall.

Ask a friend to help you hold the roof in place.

Leave a gap at the front for the entrance to the dome.

20 Now pick up your domed roof and lower it onto the wall. Make sure the tabs on both sections line up where they meet.

Press down on
each pair of tabs.

To keep them
steady while you add
tape, hold the tabs
in place with a
binder clip.

21 Tape the wall and roof section securely
together with strong tape.

Cover the tape
with paint.

22 It's time to paint your
dome den! Choose
a bright selection of colors.

You'll need a lot of
paint for each color
that you choose.

NOW TRY THIS

Add fairy lights to the roof of your den to make a starry ceiling, or turn your den into a space base, tortoise, woodland hideout, or igloo!

1 Use a sharp pencil to pierce holes through all the triangular roof tiles of your dome.

2 Take a string of battery-powered fairy lights, and push a light through each of the holes in the roof.

3 Turn the fairy lights on, and the roof of your dome will be filled with twinkling stars!

Space base
Paint your dome gray, then decorate the roof with futuristic designs. Add a satellite and an antenna to your space base.

Tortoise
First, paint the dome brown for the **shell**. Then make the **head** and **legs** and tape them to the tabs.

Woodland hideout
Decorate your dome in a green and brown camouflage pattern. Add twigs and leaves for a woodland look!

Igloo
Paint the dome in icy blue and white colors. Then stick iceberg-shaped pieces of cardboard to the outside wall.

Turn to page 61 to find out how to make a racing helmet.

Use corrugated cardboard to add grip to your tires.

RECYCLED RACER

Have you ever wanted to get behind the wheel of a race car and drive around a track at high speed? Well now you can build one that looks just like the real thing, featuring chunky tires, a wedged-shaped nose, a cockpit you can get into, and even a stylish spoiler at the back.

Wear the car on your shoulders and race your friends!

The wedge-shaped front makes your model look as sleek as a real race car.

HOW TO MAKE A
RECYCLED RACER

You need lots of cardboard and strong tape for this project. First, you'll be turning the box into the car's cockpit—the part the driver sits inside. Then you'll be using sheets of cardboard to build your car around the cockpit.

A **large-scale project** for the whole family to get involved in!

Difficulty level: Hard

YOU WILL NEED

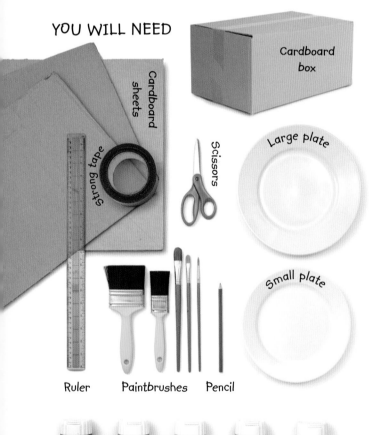

Cardboard sheets

Cardboard box

Strong tape

Scissors

Large plate

Small plate

Ruler   Paintbrushes   Pencil

Paints

Short flap

Keep the round piece you cut out.

1 To build the **cockpit**, cut a head-sized hole in the base of the box. Cut off the short flaps, too.

Backrest is twice the height of the box.

2 For the **backrest**, cut a cardboard piece twice the height of the box, with an arched top. Tape it to the side of the box as shown.

3 Cut slits into the ends of the flap from the edge of the box to the edge of the backrest. Score and fold each end to create tabs.

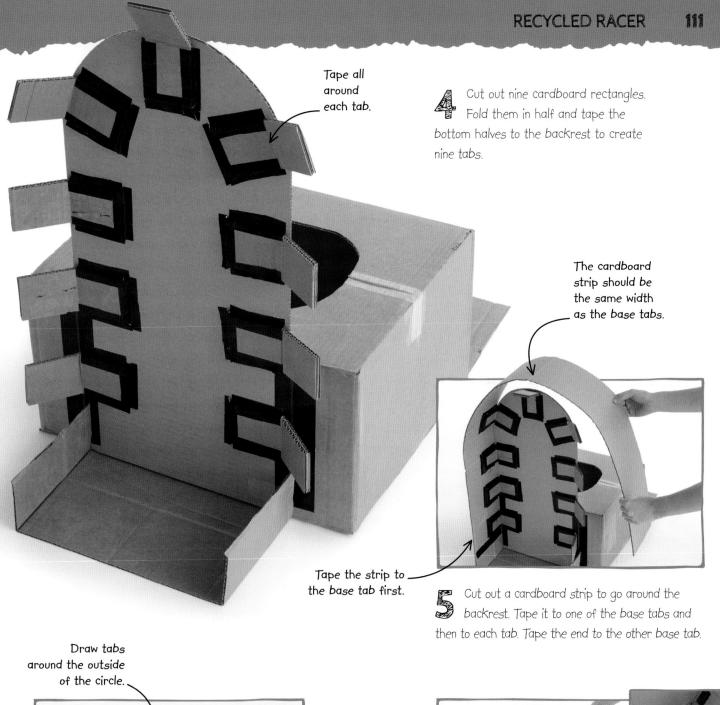

Tape all around each tab.

Tape the strip to the base tab first.

The cardboard strip should be the same width as the base tabs.

4 Cut out nine cardboard rectangles. Fold them in half and tape the bottom halves to the backrest to create nine tabs.

5 Cut out a cardboard strip to go around the backrest. Tape it to one of the base tabs and then to each tab. Tape the end to the other base tab.

Draw tabs around the outside of the circle.

6 For the **back wheels**, draw around a large plate on cardboard. Add tabs around the circle, cut it out, and fold the tabs. Repeat to make another wheel.

Cut strips out of corrugated cardboard to create tires with grip.

7 To add **tires** to the wheels, tape a thin strip of cardboard to the tabs on each wheel, then tape the ends of the strip together.

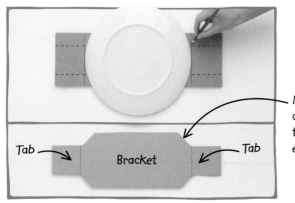

Make diagonal cuts to trim off the corners of each bracket.

Tab

Bracket

Tab

8 For the **wheel brackets**, draw around your large plate on cardboard. Add tabs to each end and cut the piece out. Repeat step to make another bracket.

Tape

Tape both tabs securely to the inside of the wheel.

9 Tape the tabs of the brackets to the inside of the back wheel. Repeat **steps 6–9** using the smaller plate to make the **front wheels**.

Use tape across wheels and base for extra support.

You'll be attaching the front wheels to the car in step 22.

10 Tape the bracket of the back wheels to each side of the backrest. Then, flip the car over and tape across the base and back wheels.

Bend the strips so they bow.

11 To add **braces**, cut a long, thin strip of cardboard and tape it from the side of the cockpit to the backrest. Fix an identical strip to the other side.

For the nose, use a sheet of cardboard that is wider than the car.

12 Now make the **nose piece**. Fold a large sheet of cardboard in half. Slide the lower half underneath the cockpit and rest the upper fold on top.

13 Hold a front wheel against the upper fold on the side of the nose piece and draw lines to mark where it sits. Repeat on the other side.

Take off the nose piece to complete marking the wheel slots.

14 Join the two lines you've drawn on each side to make two rectangles, each one wide and deep enough for the wheels to slot into.

15 Carefully cut out the wheel slots with scissors. Afterward, put the wheels into the slots to check they fit.

16 To make the car look aerodynamic, draw curves on the nose piece and in front of each wheel. Take the piece off and cut along the lines.

17 Now fold the piece in half and draw around the upper sheet to copy the shape onto the lower half. Cut along the lines so the two halves are the same.

18 To attach the nose piece to the car, fold the end of the lower half up against the front of the cockpit.

19 Tape the nose piece to the top of the cockpit and to the sides of the flap at the base of the cockpit to secure the piece to the car.

Fold the nose piece over the cockpit.

20 Fold the upper part of the nose piece over so it rests on top of the cockpit. This will cover part of the hole where your head goes.

Cut away the marked area to clear the cockpit hole.

21 Place the oval piece you cut out in **step 1** over the cockpit hole. Draw around it to mark the part covering the hole, then cut it out.

22 Tape the upper fold to the top of the cockpit. The nose piece should now fit perfectly around the cockpit hole.

23 To secure the front wheels, slot them in place first. Then lay a cardboard strip at the front and mark the distance between the inner wheel rims.

24 Fold the strip along the markings to create tabs. Place the strip on the nose between the wheels, so the tabs align with the wheel brackets.

25 Tape the strip to the top of the car. Trim the tab ends if necessary, then tape them to the wheel brackets.

26 To add the **spoiler**, cut a cardboard strip the same length as the car's width. Hold it against the backrest and mark the slit points.

Trim the corners on one side to create the **spoiler shape.**

27 Now cut the slits, ensuring that they are long enough for the spoiler to slot securely into place without touching the braces. Slide the piece in.

Number plate

Screen visor

28 Now you can add details to your car such as a **screen visor** or a circular **number plate** for the front of the car.

29 Well done! You've built your race car. It's time to make it look fabulous by painting it in bold colors.

WILD MASKS

Get ready to tap into your wild side! With these impressive lion and zebra masks, you can dress up as two of nature's most majestic animals. The masks are ideal for a safari-themed party, or a game of chase where the lion's aim is to catch the nimble-footed zebra.

HOW TO MAKE A
LION MASK

You can either get a friend to help you *build* the mask around your head or *build* it on a balloon stand. If you decide to make a stand, blow up a balloon to roughly the size of your head and place it on a round cardboard base about the same width as your neck. This will help you make sure your mask fits you perfectly.

Take your time. Your patience will be rewarded.

Difficulty level: Hard

YOU WILL NEED

Paintbrushes

Strong tape

Paints

Scissors

Pencil

Glue

Ruler

Cardboard sheets

Front

Tape the stand to your work surface.

1 First, make the **frame** of the mask. Cut four strips of cardboard long enough to wrap around your head. Wrap the first strip around the middle of the balloon.

2 Wrap a second strip over the top of the balloon, so the ends are level with the base of the balloon stand. Tape the second strip securely to the first.

3 Wrap a third strip diagonally across the back of the stand so it overlaps the first two strips. Tape it to the two strips on each side as shown.

Lower jaw

4 Loop a fourth strip across the front of the mask, positioning the ends over the third strip on each side. The fourth strip will form the lion's **lower jaw**.

5 Tape the ends of the lower jaw strip securely in place on both sides. The frame of the lion mask is now complete!

6 To make the **muzzle**, draw a rectangle about three times wider than the width of the balloon. Mark it into three equal sections.

7 Draw gentle curves across the base of each section. Then draw curves to round off the upper corners at each end. Cut the muzzle out.

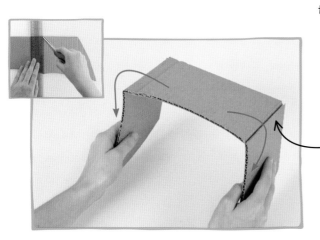

8 Use the blunt tip of your scissors to score along the two dividing lines and fold the ends down to create an n-shaped muzzle piece.

The width of the muzzle should roughly match the width of the mask's frame.

The middle section of the muzzle should form a curved shape.

9 Position the muzzle at the front of the mask and tape the ends to the sides of the jaw strip. The top of the muzzle should be slightly curved.

You may need to alter the size of the template to make a nose piece that matches the width of your muzzle.

10 For the **nose**, copy the template on page 143 and draw around it on cardboard. Flip the template over and draw around it again.

11 Cut the piece out. Score the ends and fold them to make tabs. Then position the nose across the muzzle and tape the tabs to either side.

The mouth piece should look like this once you've cut it out.

12 For the **mouth**, cut a strip of cardboard long enough to wrap around the jaw of your mask. Fold it in half, draw the shape above, and cut it out.

13 Bend the mouth piece into a curved shape, folding in the bumpy edge to create the lion mask's bottom lip.

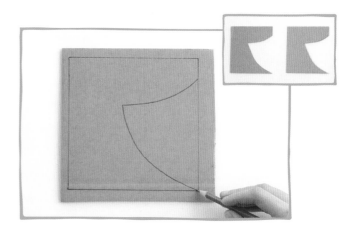

14 Tuck the mouth piece into the inside of the lower jaw with the bumpy edge facing up. Tape it to the jaw from the inside to secure.

15 For the **brows**, draw a curved triangle inside a cardboard square and cut it out. Draw around the shape to create a second, identical piece.

16 Tape the brows to either side of the mask at the top of the frame. Make sure the pointed ends are facing the front.

Tape the brow to the frame.

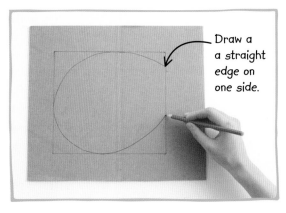

Draw a a straight edge on one side.

17 For the **cheeks**, draw an oval shape large enough to cover the sides of the mask from the muzzle to base of the brow. Cut the piece out.

Tape the straight edge of the cheek to the muzzle.

18 Draw around the piece to make the other cheek and cut it out. Tape the cheeks to either side of the mask.

Trim along the outline of the arrowhead to make tabs with diagonal edges.

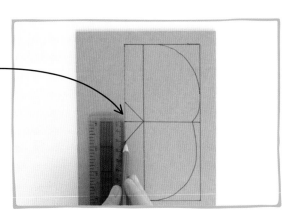

19 For the **ears**, draw a B inside two squares. Add a vertical line along one edge for tabs and an arrowhead across the central line. Cut the piece out.

Turn one ear over before you score and fold it, so the ears mirror each other.

20 Draw around the piece to make the other ear and cut it out. Score and fold each ear along the horizontal and vertical lines.

21 Tape the tabs of the ears to the brow pieces on either side of the mask. Tape the top of the ears to the brow pieces too.

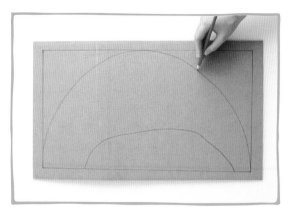

22 For the **mane**, draw a large crescent on cardboard, making it long enough to stretch from the lower jaw to the brow of the mask.

23 Cut out the shape. Then lay it on a piece of cardboard and trace around it to draw an identical piece. Cut this piece out too.

24 Bend each half of the mane into a curved shape before attaching it to the mask. If necessary, trim the inner curve for a better fit.

Tape the mane piece to the inside of the lower jaw.

25 Attach the mane pieces to either side of the mask by taping the ends to the brow pieces and lower jaw.

26 It's time to decorate your mask! Paint the mane in red and the rest of the mask in orange. Let the paint dry.

27 To complete the mane, paint a large cardboard sheet in red, orange, and yellow. Once the paint dries, cut the sheet into thin strips.

28 Glue the strips to the mane, spreading the colors evenly around the mask. Curl the ends of the strips to make the mane *big* and *bushy*.

29 Now add the **whiskers**. Cut out six cardboard strips with tapered ends and paint them white. Glue them to the nose as shown.

30 Your lion mask is ready to wear! Because you've tailored the mask to the size of your head, it should fit perfectly.

HOW TO MAKE A
ZEBRA MASK

The frame of the zebra mask is exactly the same as that of the lion mask. Once again, build the frame around your head, or on a balloon stand that roughly matches the size of your head. Then add the zebra's long nose, ears, and mane.

YOU WILL NEED

Paintbrushes

Strong tape

Cardboard sheets

Scissors

Black and white paint

Pencil

Glue

Ruler

With **fewer pieces to cut,** this mask should be quicker to build.

Difficulty level:
Medium

Forehead

Jaw

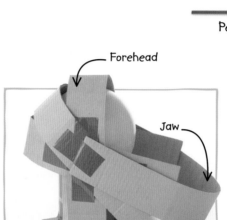

This line should be as wide as your head.

Draw the dotted lines.

1 Make the **frame** of your zebra mask out of four cardboard strips, following **steps 1–4 of the lion mask.**

2 For the zebra's **nose,** draw the above shape on cardboard, adding the dotted lines, and cut the piece out.

Front of nose.

Draw three tabs at the base.

3 Fold the sides of the nose along the dotted lines. Then bend the front section into a curved shape.

4 Flip the nose piece over and tape it to the sides of the jaw strip, making sure the curve is at the front.

5 For the **ears,** draw the above shape with tabs at the base and cut it out. Draw around it to make an identical ear.

6 Bend the ear from both ends and bring the bottom corners together to form a funnel shape.

7 Fold out the three tabs at the base. Wrap tape around the ear, above the tabs, to secure the shape.

8 Tape the tabs of the ear to one side of the forehead strip. Repeat **steps 6–8** to add the other ear.

The inner rim needs be long enough to span the back of the mask.

Paint the ears white first and add the black stripes afterward.

9 For the **mane**, draw a crescent on cardboard. Add tabs to the ends of the inner rim. Cut the shape out.

10 Fold the tabs in opposite directions from each other and tape them onto the mask to attach the mane.

11 Finally, paint your mask black (except the ears) and let it dry. Then, paint on the white stripes. Paint the ears white and add black stripes.

Paint a white stripe around each nostril.

Leave the end of the jaw black for the zebra's mouth.

PIRATE SHIP

Transform a cardboard box into this magnificent ship, with tall masts and billowing sails. You can even make swashbuckling pirates and stand them on deck, ready for adventures and fun at sea!

Topsail

Cross spars

Main sails

Lower spars

Lower sails

Jib sails

Bowsprit

HOW TO MAKE A
PIRATE SHIP

Once you've turned a cardboard box into a sturdy structure for your ship, you'll be using lots of cardboard and wooden sticks to add masts, sails, and cannons. Make sure you know what all the different parts of the ship are called—the picture on the opposite page will help you!

You'll need to **measure your sails against the masts** for a perfect fit.

Difficulty level:
Hard

YOU WILL NEED

Wooden sticks, painted black

Paintbrushes

Strong tape

String

Adhesive putty

Paint

Glue

Pencil

Scissors

Cardboard sheet

Medium box

1 Draw a three-sided shape at the top of the box. Then draw a curve across one lower corner for the front of the ship and a diagonal line across the other for the rear.

Don't throw away the piece you cut out.

2 Extend the three-sided shape across the top of the box and copy it on the other side. Then cut it out and set it aside.

Draw lines from the top of your shapes across the width of the box.

3 Cut along the curve and diagonal line you have drawn, then cut around the edges to make two holes as shown.

The curve must match the one on the other side of the box.

4 Turn the box around and line up the cut-outs with the markings across its width. Draw around them to create identical shapes.

5 Cut along all the marked sections to complete the ship's **structure**.

The tubes need to be taller than the ship's structure.

6 To make the **masts** and **cannons**, roll five strips of cardboard into tight tubes and secure the edges with tape, making sure they are taller than the ship's structure. Paint them all black.

Rear deck

7 On the inner edge of the rear deck, draw around a tube and cut out the hole. Dab glue on the bottom of the tube. Push it into the hole and stick it to the ship's base, so it stands straight up.

8 Use your cut-out from **step 2** as the **main deck platform**. Place another tube near the edge of the platform, draw a circle around the tube, and cut the hole out.

Front deck

9 Fold over the sides of the platform and dab glue onto them, then stick them to the inside of the ship's structure. The hole on the platform should be near the front deck.

10 Dab glue onto the bottom of the tube. Then push it into the hole to stick it to the ship's base. Your two masts are now in place.

Use a ruler to make sure the dots are in the same place on both sides.

11 Use a pencil to mark three evenly spaced dots on the ship's side for the cannons. Mark dots in the same place on the other side.

Draw around the tube over all six dots.

12 Take another tube from **step 6** and draw around it where the dots are marked. Cut out the six holes that you have drawn.

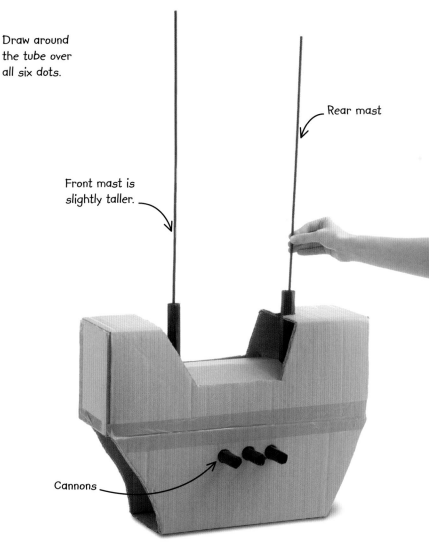

Front mast is slightly taller.

Rear mast

Cannons

13 Push the remaining three tubes from **step 6** through the holes in the ship and out the other side. You have now made the ship's cannons.

14 To finish the masts, take two thin wooden sticks about the same height as your ship. Stick them into the cardboard tubes.

Bowsprit

15 To add the **bowsprit**, pierce a hole into the front of the ship using a pencil. Then push a wooden stick into the hole, pointing up at a slight angle.

17 Paint the circles and strips of cardboard black on both sides. Once the paint has dried, dab glue all along one side of each strip.

19 Slide one of your circles down the rear mast so that it sits on top of the base. Repeat the process for the front mast.

Use adhesive putty to protect your fingers.

16 Now, make the **crow's nests**. Cut out two strips of cardboard and two small circles. Put adhesive putty on one side, then use a sharp pencil to pierce a hole in the center of each circle.

Make sure there is enough space for the sails above and below the crow's nests.

18 To make **bases** for the crow's nests, coil a strip from **step 17** around the rear mast about halfway up, with the glue on the inside. Repeat this on the front mast, slightly lower down.

Cross spar

20 Now add the first **cross spar**. Hold a short wooden stick across the front mast (slightly below the top) and secure it with tape.

21 Repeat step 20 to add another cross spar to the front mast, and a cross spar to the rear mast.

Add the second cross spar a third of the way down the front mast.

Add a cross spar slightly below the top of the rear mast.

Lower spars should point to the rear of the ship.

22 Add the **lower spars** by taping short wooden sticks below each crow's nest base, at right angles to the masts.

Make your sails taller than the spaces between the spars and crow's nests so they will curve out.

23 Cut out two identical cardboard rectangles for the **main sails** and a slightly smaller one for the **topsail**. Cut small grooves the same width as the wooden sticks into each sail as shown.

Jib sail

24 To make the **lower sails**, cut out two cardboard rectangles. Line them up against the lower spars and mark the angle of the spars and where they sit. Cut along these lines.

25 To make the **jib sails**, cut out two triangular cardboard shapes as shown that fit between the bowsprit and the front mast.

26 Now paint your ship. Apply a base coat of brown paint to the ship's structure. Let it dry, and then paint on the details.

27 Paint red and white stripes on your seven sails and let them dry.

Pierce holes to thread the string through.

28 Pierce holes into either corner of the longest edge of the jib sails. Then thread string through each hole and along the side of the sails as shown.

29 Pierce holes into both top corners and the bottom left corner of the lower sails. Thread a short piece of string through each hole.

30 Now secure your sails to the ship. First, take your jib sails and tie the string to the bowsprit and front mast.

31 Tie the top of the lower sails to the lower spars. Then tie the bottom left corner to each of the ship's masts.

Make more flags
by gluing paper
triangles to
the mast tops.

Pierce a hole in
the ship's rear,
and slide your
flag into position.

32 Now attach the main sails and topsail to the masts. Bend the sails into curved shapes and use the grooves to hook them onto the masts.

33 Finally, make your **flag**. Paint a skull and crossbones onto a piece of cardboard, with tabs as shown above, and glue it to a short wooden stick.

NOW TRY THIS

Make a **crew** for your ship. Draw pirates on cardboard, using the templates on page 144. Cut slits in the base of the pirates and use a folded strip of cardboard to stand them up.

Fold the strip for
the stand in half.

Slot the ends
through the slits.

TEMPLATES

To make your own template, lay a piece of plain paper over the required shape and trace it fully, making sure you include any detail. Cut your template out, place it on cardboard and trace the outline before drawing on the details as accurately as you can.

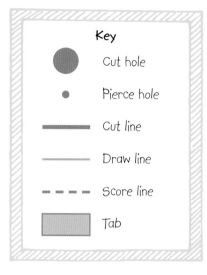

Key

● Cut hole

• Pierce hole

━━━ Cut line

─── Draw line

- - - Score line

� Tab

Ring Toss Challenge P.20

Balancing Butterflies P.24

Funky Flowers P.32

Racing Rabbits

Spinner P.49

Racing Rabbits—Rabbits P.48

Racing Rabbits—Kangaroo P.49

Puppet Dragon—Wing P.54

Puppet Dragon—Head P.53

Puppet Dragon—Fang P.52

Puppet Dragon—Tail P.53

Puppet Dragon—Whisker P.52

Puppet Dragon—Tongue P.52

Hero's Helmet P.59

Tropical Aquarium P.72

Adventure Castle P.87

Adventure Castle

Adventure Castle

Pharaoh's Finery—Pendant P.76

Pharaoh's Finery—Scarab P.77

Pharaoh's Finery—Crown   P.78

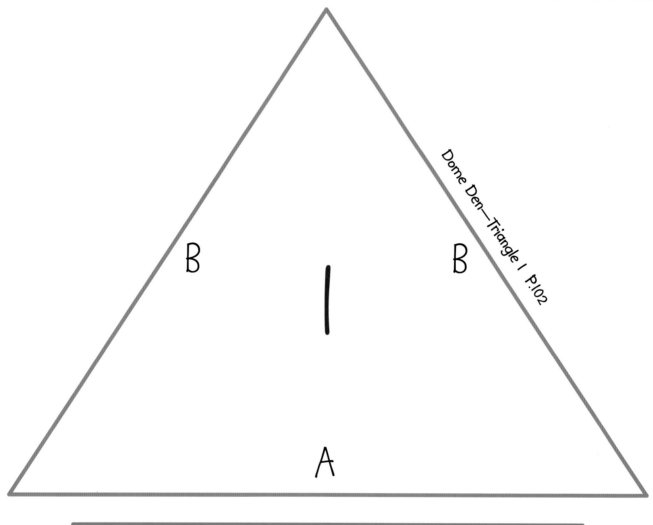

Dome Den—Triangle 1 P.102

B

B

I

A

Penguin Family P.90

Overlap area for stand

Foot

Scarf

Wing

Beak

Wing

Scarf

Foot

Overlap area for stand

Foot slit

Foot slit

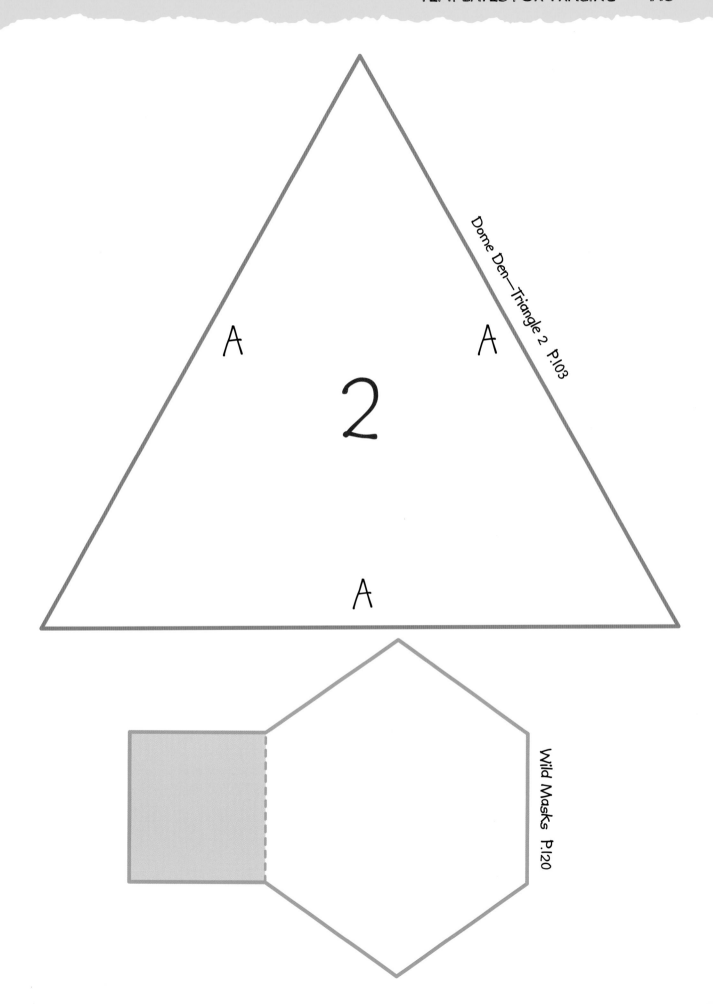

Dome Den—Triangle 2 P.103

A

A

2

A

Wild Masks P.120

Pirate Ship P.133

ACKNOWLEDGMENTS

The publisher would like to thank the following people for their assistance in the preparation of this book:
Andrew Bishop, Adam Brackenbury, Steve Crozier, Phil Fitzgerald, Tom Morse, and Stefan Podhorodecki for retouching;
Gary Ombler and Howard Shooter for additional photography; Michelle Baxter, Laura Gardner, Karen Self, and Sharon
Spencer for additional photography art direction; Amanda Learmonth for proofreading; Mason Beacher, Eliana Burchell,
Jessica Cawthra, Kit Lane, Helen Leech, Priscilla Nelson-Cole, James Self, Kaiya Shang, Chloe Shooter, Luke Shooter,
Oliver Shooter, and Jemma Westing for modeling; Felix Belfield and Jasmine Parker for assistance with the Cardville
City project.

Note from the author
Thank you to the following people for their creative support and great patience over the years: Jeanette Sutton,
John Archer, Scott Westing, Sophie Elder, the BrilliantBuilds crew, and, of course, my mum and dad.